"Amid the avalanche of books on preaching, this one is really worth reading. With his trademark clarity and care, David Jackman gives us principles for preaching that are genuinely biblical, together with specific examples that enable the reader to see what this looks like in practice. His practical advice on how to approach a text and produce an effective sermon is invaluable. Jackman is a master teacher of preaching, and all who read this book will be refreshed in their appreciation of the task and strengthened in a faithful ministry of the written word of God."

Mark D. Thompson, Principal, Moore Theological College

"Here is a book for every preacher to own, read, and digest. David Jackman distills a lifetime of experience as a preacher, a teacher of preachers worldwide, and a pastor to preachers. As we would expect from Jackman, the book is crystal clear in its instruction, abundantly well illustrated in its examples, and deeply biblical in its content. It also breathes the warm heart of one who knows what it is to struggle with preaching and to encourage others in this work. I particularly love chapter 16 with its guidance on the appropriate tones for preaching; only an experienced pastor could write this as Jackman does. I am so grateful to him for writing this book."

Christopher Ash, Writer in Residence, Tyndale House, Cambridge; Former Director, Cornhill Training Course; author, *The Priority of Preaching*

"Here, surely, is the Bible expositor's indispensable companion from a trustworthy and seasoned practitioner who takes us step-by-step, patiently but unequivocally, through the nuts and bolts of expository preaching, showing us best practices to emulate and pitfalls to avoid. Throughout the book, the timeless authority of the Bible as the word of God for all of life is strongly affirmed. No investment can be too much for this long-awaited classic."

Emmanuel A. S. Egbunu, Bishop of Lokoja, Church of Nigeria

"A gem of a preaching manual by a master preacher and trainer. Give this to your pastor to encourage him to keep on keeping on. Give it to your trainees so that they learn to stay on the line. May David Jackman's lifetime of wisdom as an expositor and trainer of expositors bless you as I have been so richly blessed by his training over the years."

Denesh Divyanathan, Senior Pastor, The Crossing Church, Singapore; Chairman, Evangelical Theological College of Asia; President, Project Timothy Singapore

"By the grace of God, David Jackman has trained numerous faithful preachers, who in turn have gone on to train others with the things they have learned through him. This book encapsulates his teaching with clarity and conviction, making it an invaluable resource for preachers and their trainers. May the Lord raise up many more faithful expositors of his word from around the world, and may this excellent tool be widely used as part of that process."

Andrew Cheah, Dean, St. Mary's Anglican Cathedral, Kuala Lumpur, Malaysia

"David Jackman has devoted much of his ministry to training the next generation of preachers. The Lord has multiplied his labors at the Proclamation Trust in London to benefit churches across Great Britain and around the world. This book represents his distilled wisdom and instruction on the subject of preaching—and it is a treasure trove. From start to finish it is marked by biblical clarity, practical help, and pastoral warmth. Would-be preachers ought to read this book carefully at the outset of ministry, and serving pastors would do well to sharpen their skills by taking time to heed Jackman's guidance. This book is a gift to the church."

Jonathan Griffiths, Lead Pastor, The Metropolitan Bible Church, Ottawa, Canada

"David Jackman equips those in the church and the academy with a deep and clear handbook for expository preaching. *Proclaiming the Word* delivers principles and practices saturated with Christian character and wisdom for the long haul."

Theo Karvounakis, Director and Professor of Theology, Greek Bible College

"David Jackman is a much-esteemed leader in the conservative evangelical movement in England and beyond. His experience in pastoral ministry and training others for pastoral ministry shines through this book. Jackman is ideally suited to provide not just encouragement or exhortation but also a training manual for future generations of preachers. In this book you will find a tonic toward a fresh commitment to expository preaching. You will also be given realistic and helpful tools to develop as a preacher. *Proclaiming the Word* is practical, encouraging, biblical, and challenging."

Josh Moody, Senior Pastor, College Church, Wheaton, Illinois; President, God Centered Life Ministries

"I don't know a better trainer of preachers than David Jackman, so I am delighted that his teaching has now been made widely available in this book. It will be a great help, both to novices and experienced practitioners alike."

Vaughan Roberts, Rector, St Ebbe's, Oxford, United Kingdom

"This is a book for beginners and for veterans. David Jackman has tutored many in the art of preaching. His work is clear but not simplistic; it is principled and also practical. Above all, it is biblical, expounding the relevant texts so that we can see what God wants of us when we preach. At many points, I found it deeply challenging as I considered my own long-established habits in the light of the author's wisdom. I hope that it will be widely read."

Peter Jensen, former Archbishop of Sydney

"This is an empowering book. David Jackman, as always, is clear, thoughtful, and persuasive. This book journeys through biblical convictions, the realities preachers face, and both the mindset and skill set needed to grow as a preacher of God's word. With years of experience condensed in a single volume, this resource is a great gift to anyone in the church seeking to develop as an expositor of the Bible."

Nat Schluter, Principal, Johannesburg Bible College

"In this excellent book, David Jackman distills a lifetime of wisdom as both an expository preacher and a teacher of expository preaching. Here you have an overview of the preacher's task, an explanation of the skills required, and worked examples to put those principles into practice. It is a guide for new preachers, a textbook on preaching, and a repository of tools for the practiced preacher. This is a great gift to the church that all expository Bible preachers will want to have at hand for the great work entrusted to them."

Justyn Terry, Vice Principal and Academic Dean, Wycliffe Hall, Oxford

Proclaiming the Word

Proclaiming the Word

Principles and Practices for
Expository Preaching

David J. Jackman

Foreword by Peter Nicholas

WHEATON, ILLINOIS

Proclaiming the Word: Principles and Practices for Expository Preaching
© 2024 by David J. Jackman
Published by Crossway
    1300 Crescent Street
    Wheaton, Illinois 60187

Cover design: Jordan Singer
First printing 2024
Printed in the United States of America

Trade paperback ISBN: 978-1-4335-9210-2
ePub ISBN: 978-1-4335-9212-6
PDF ISBN: 978-1-4335-9211-9

Library of Congress Cataloging-in-Publication Data

Names: Jackman, David, author. | Nicholas, Peter, contributor.
Title: Proclaiming the word : principles and practices for expository preaching / David J. Jackman ; a foreword by Peter Nicholas.
Description: Wheaton, Illinois : Crossway, 2024. | Includes bibliographical references and index.
Identifiers: LCCN 2023042756 (print) | LCCN 2023042757 (ebook) | ISBN 9781433592102 (trade paperback) | ISBN 9781433592119 (pdf) | ISBN 9781433592126 (e-pub)
Subjects: LCSH: Preaching. | Exposition (Rhetoric)—Religious aspects.
Classification: LCC BV4211.3 .J33 2024 (print) | LCC BV4211.3 (ebook) | DDC 251—dc23/eng/20240213
LC record available at https://lccn.loc.gov/2023042756
LC ebook record available at https://lccn.loc.gov/2023042757

Crossway is a publishing ministry of Good News Publishers.

| BP | | 33 | 32 | 31 | 30 | 29 | 28 | 27 | 26 | 25 | 24 |
| 15 | 14 | 13 | 12 | 11 | 10 | 9 | 8 | 7 | 6 | 5 | 4 | 3 | 2 | 1 |

Contents

Foreword

IN EVERY GENERATION, preaching has its detractors. In this generation, cases for abandoning preaching range from declining attention spans in those brought up on TikTok, to sermons being elitist because they only appeal to the college educated who have learned to sit through lectures, to a preference for discussion instead of being "preached at" due to postmodernity's antiauthoritarian bias.

And yet, something unique about preaching appeals to all cultures and gives it enduring significance even today—in fact, especially today. Whether in a rural community in Uganda or with university students in New York, there is something leveling and accessible across varying contexts about a person standing up and giving a sustained monologue to a community of listeners. A brief survey of history will show even the casual observer that this simple but vital mode of communication transcends class, culture, education, and life experience. How wise the Lord is to choose this as his primary mode to teach his people and to share good news with those who do not yet follow Christ!

The challenge that we face in our day and age is not that preaching has ceased to be relevant but that our confidence in preaching is shaken and our practice of preaching lacks conviction and skill to engage an increasingly post-Christian landscape. Those are the two elements that need to be constantly refreshed: *conviction* and *skill*. For while God may be the only one who can ensure that people are "cut to the heart" (Acts 2:37) and that the sermon lands with power and with the Holy Spirit (1 Thess. 1:5), our responsibility as preachers lies in these twin areas:

- *Conviction* so that the preacher dwells in the word and the word dwells in the preacher;
- *Skill* to mine the text, diagnose the relevant dispositions of the human heart, target God's message into the cultural context, and communicate in a way that brings all this together and connects with those listening.

It is all too easy for preachers to lament that the Holy Spirit does not seem to be at work in the way we hoped he would be when we have not fulfilled our role in a convinced and skillfully delivered sermon.

For these reasons, this book is a must-read both for those beginning this high calling and for more established preachers. Having had the privilege of calling David a mentor for a number of years, I know firsthand his rare ability both to engender a deep conviction that God works through the preaching of his word and to demystify and train preachers in the tools wielded by God's workman. David has been training students in preaching for a remarkable thirty years. He has encouraged and equipped people of different ages, stages, ethnicities, nationalities, and backgrounds. Having this material now honed into a book (something many of us were praying would happen) is a rare gift to the church, and I pray it will bless you as it has so many others.

By way of briefly seeking to bolster your conviction that preaching is a high calling even today, I want to refer to a small book written in 1592 by the Puritan William Perkins, *The Art of Prophesying* (i.e., preaching), a book I heard David refer to many years ago and one that I subsequently read. In his preface, Perkins argued that effective preaching has three benefits alongside the evangelistic dynamic of "gathering the church and bringing together all of the elect":

1. "It drives away wolves from the folds of the Lord."
2. It allures our souls away from ungodliness to follow Christ.
3. It is "the weapon which has shaken the foundations of ancient heresies."[1]

Each of these three statements draws on a different picture that illuminates an important aspect of preaching and points to the multifaceted nature of the sermon and the preacher who delivers it.

The first image speaks of the preacher in that familiar role of shepherd. As Psalm 23 reminds us, a shepherd uses both a rod and a staff (Ps. 23:4): a rod to drive away the predators (supremely the world, the flesh, and the devil) who unchecked would ravage the flock and a staff to draw wandering sheep back into the fold tenderly. Some preachers by disposition are more naturally tender and comforting. Others are better at correcting and confronting. A wise shepherd of the flock will recognize the need for both as we follow the true shepherd who is "full of grace and truth" (John 1:14).

The second image communicates something of the aesthetic of the gospel and the preacher as the artist seeking to represent this beauty with deft brushstrokes. Thomas Cranmer has been summarized as teaching, "What the heart loves, the will chooses, and the mind justifies."[2] Therefore, to preach Christ is to represent his beauty before the eyes of those listening such that they yearn to know him better and are drawn to love him more deeply.

From shepherd to artist and, finally, to a soldier, the third image represents that familiar mode, though perhaps unpopular today, of the fight in the Christian life. To preach is to wield the very sword of the Spirit, which is the word of God, recognizing that our battle is not

---

1   William Perkins, *The Art of Prophesying: And the Calling of the Ministry* (repr., Edinburgh, UK: Banner of Truth, 2021). Available online at https://www.monergism.com/thethreshold/sdg/perkins _prophesying.html.

2   Summarized by Ashley Null. I have heard him use this phrase numerous times in person and in talks.

against flesh and blood but against the rulers and authorities in the heavenly realms (see Eph. 6:12–17). Therefore, the preacher's weapons are not the weapons of this world, but have "divine power to demolish strongholds . . . and every pretension that sets itself up against the knowledge of God" (2 Cor. 10:4–5).

Shepherd, artist, and soldier. I hope that you see how varied and multifaceted the preacher's calling is! If you feel a little daunted, as I do, then I know this book will assuage your fears and equip you to use the right tool in the right way and at the right time—whether the shepherd's rod and staff, the artist's paintbrush, or the soldier's sword.

Equally, though, I hope that your pulse has quickened a bit and that a sense of the glory of this calling fills you with hope and expectancy: hope that God can work through you, weak and sinful as you are, and expectancy about what he may do in and through you as you give yourself to this ministry. *Soli Deo gloria!*

Rev. Peter Nicholas
SENIOR PASTOR
REDEEMER DOWNTOWN, NEW YORK CITY, NEW YORK

Preface

FOR THE PAST THIRTY YEARS, I have been engaged in training preachers for expository ministry under the auspices of the Proclamation Trust. It has been my privilege to work with many young preachers, coming alongside to help them improve their Bible handling abilities, cultivate essential skills, and develop their practical experience in proclaiming the word. The Trust was founded in 1986 to propagate expository preaching in thankfulness for the outstandingly effective ministry of Dick Lucas over twenty-five years (at that time) as rector of the church of St. Helen, Bishopsgate, in London. The Cornhill Training Course, of which I was the first director, is a ministry of the Trust, which God has used in the UK and in similar initiatives in other parts of the world. The basics that Dick Lucas taught us forty years ago have always been at the heart of this ministry, and revisiting them has provided renewed stimulus for this present work.

The book is structured as three modules, each exploring from different angles both the development of the expository sermon, or talk, and that of the expository preacher. Moving through the basic necessities of biblical preaching and the fundamentals of how to go about the task, the first module also addresses the preacher's own convictions, commitment, and personal development. The second module looks in more detail at the range of practical skills to be identified and practiced as the basic tools for the task. Finally, the third module focuses on preaching Scripture as the whole counsel of God, along with the rewards of patient persistence in this privileged calling.

Obviously, this is not the sort of book to be read through at a sitting or two, although a body of knowledge and experience should accumulate as the chapters unfold. Rather, it has the character of a hands-on training manual, where each chapter has a specific role to play in assembling the bigger picture. The aim is to identify and illustrate biblically the principles and methodology of exposition so that the reader can have confidence that such preaching is dependent on and actively shaped by the word of God. Working through the book, there is some occasional and intentional repetition. Significant points can benefit through reinforcement from a variety of different contexts. Convictions are often strengthened and skills developed by a drip feed approach rather than an overload of information. There is also an important pastoral element designed to nurture the preacher, not just as a competent practitioner, but as a faithful disciple and obedient servant of the Lord Jesus Christ. Timothy was exhorted to keep a close watch on his life as well as his teaching (1 Tim. 4:16).

My prayer is that the contents of these chapters may help to stimulate and equip a new generation of Bible expositors, engaging in the adventure of becoming "a worker who has no need to be ashamed, rightly handling the word of truth" (2 Tim. 2:15). But this book is not just for those starting out! No matter how long we have been preaching, we all need to return to the training camp from time to time to renew our enthusiasm, sharpen our skills, increase our proficiency, and deepen our dedication. There is no more urgent task today and no greater privilege than to dedicate our time and talents to the faithful proclamation of God's revealed truth—the whole truth and nothing but the truth. "Therefore, having this ministry by the mercy of God, we do not lose heart" (2 Cor. 4:1).

David Jackman
EASTBOURNE, ENGLAND
OCTOBER 2023

Acknowledgments

I AM INDEBTED TO so many colleagues and students who have helped me over the past thirty years to clarify and develop the principles and practices this book contains. It has been an immense privilege to work through these concepts with hundreds of students on the Cornhill Training Course in London and its offshoots elsewhere, as well as with many pastors and preachers around the world in training workshops for expository preaching. In all of these situations, I have been a learner as much as a teacher, and I am so grateful for all those who have helped me personally through their engagement and feedback.

Several years ago, many of these basic principles were brought together in a series of training videos titled "Equipped to Preach the Word," for which I remain very grateful to Sam Shammas, whose editorial and production skills were so formative and whose enthusiasm for the materials was positively infectious. I wish also to express my appreciation of the diligence and hard work put into the typing of the manuscript by Nancy Olsen, my friend and colleague of many years, for her special skills in deciphering my hieroglyphics and without whom this book would not have seen the light of day.

I am grateful to the whole team at Crossway, especially to Todd Augustine for his interest and support in developing the project and to my editor Chris Cowan for his patience and his many insightful comments and suggestions, which have shaped and so much improved the final version. To them and to all the Crossway staff, who have given me such consistent support and encouragement, I express my sincere gratitude and appreciation.

Finally, I am, as always, so thankful for my wonderful wife of fifty-four years, Heather, for her constant support and encouragement in this task, which has occupied many hours of "retirement" but which is so dear to both of our hearts. Her love, wisdom, and perseverance have been a rock to me throughout my ministry. I am constantly thankful both to her and to the Lord.

Above all I thank God for the greatest privilege of involvement in the ongoing ministry of his living and enduring word, and I pray that in his hands these few crumbs may be multiplied to help raise up and equip a new generation of expository preachers around the world who will be unashamed workers, rightly handling the word of truth.

PART 1

BASIC PRINCIPLES

1

Why Does Preaching Matter?

TO MANY PEOPLE, preaching seems strangely out of place in the modern world. Why would anyone choose to go to a church building, week by week, to hear a preacher (often the same person) deliver a monologue for twenty or thirty minutes (sometimes even longer) about an ancient book with characters who lived, at best, two thousand years ago? This doesn't happen in any other context. Educational methods are increasingly interactive. Learning by discovery is the watchword. Preaching seems to be just another example of the church being out of touch, out of date, and out of steam.

Of course, it's not difficult to find examples of preaching that are sadly boring or irrelevant. Nor is it hard to hear arguments put forward to claim that preaching has had its day: we live in a visual-learning culture, listeners have sound-bite levels of concentration, study groups or one-to-one mentoring is more effective, moderns are opposed to domination of a congregation from an elevated pulpit, and so on. But the remedy for the disappointing level of much contemporary preaching is not less preaching, nor its removal from the church's agenda, but *better* preaching. And that is because something happens through preaching that cannot occur in any other communication context.

God is committed to preaching, by which he speaks through the proclamation and explanation of his word. So the preacher's task and privilege is, in J. I. Packer's memorable phrase, "to mediate a meeting with God."[1] Preaching matters not because human beings decide that it does but because through preaching God speaks today. His voice is heard. So let's look at three basic convictions or principles (and key Scripture passages for each) that help us to understand not just why preaching matters but why it is of supreme importance.

1. Preaching Matters Because the God of the Bible Is a Speaking God

The act of preaching today cannot be separated from the word of God that he has infallibly spoken in the Scriptures—the sixty-six books of divine revelation that make up our Bible. That is the bedrock foundation on which all preaching is to be built.

A basic biblical definition of the preacher is that he is a herald or proclaimer. It's a significant description because it implies that there is a message, or declaration, that the messenger is to pass on faithfully and accurately without distortion. Because God has spoken in his word, the preacher can and must preach. Without that divinely given biblical content, all that a preacher can achieve is the expression of his own, often highly questionable, opinions. On offer, then, are the mere words of human beings. They may appear attractive and promise all sorts of comfort and joy, but ultimately, they are just human words—transient and powerless. Instead, in biblical expository preaching, the authentic voice of God is heard. What is expected is that God will speak to our souls through the human agency of the preacher.

To mediate a meeting with God will require the preacher's disciplined preparation and dependence on the Holy Spirit. The conviction that such a meeting is God's purpose and, therefore, possible will have

---

1 J. I. Packer, *Truth and Power: The Place of Scripture in the Christian Life* (Downers Grove, IL: InterVarsity Press, 1999), 120.

constant implications for the preacher. If we are to be expositors, we must take sufficient time for preparation so that we have more than just a surface acquaintance with the text. We must read and reread, to listen carefully and hard, if we are to represent God's truth faithfully. This will ensure that what we say is accurate to both the content and tone of the Bible passage we are preaching. Otherwise, we may easily lead our hearers astray. We must be actively depending on God, the Holy Spirit, to grant illumination and understanding to us and our hearers so that in our preparation we are governed by his life-giving word and praying for its impact on all who hear. Equally, we must be dependent on the Spirit who inspired the text to give us clear thinking, a warm heart, and effective delivery in the process of preaching so that the wind of God may be in the sails of the sermon.

Convictions such as these need to be rooted in us through the power of the Scriptures themselves. So it will be profitable to examine a key passage from Paul in 2 Timothy to help us ensure that our view of preaching is shaped by God's word and not contemporary opinions.

At the end of his life Paul passes on the ministry baton to Timothy, who is serving as pastor-teacher in Ephesus, the church in which Paul himself had spent his longest period of settled ministry. Like many pastors today, Timothy is struggling against false teaching bringing divisive factions into the church, but the conviction Paul wants his young colleague to embrace is that the Scriptures—what he calls "the sacred writings"—are more than sufficient as his authoritative source of divine revelation by which he can fulfill his ministry and lead the church. Paul writes, "But as for you, continue in what you have learned and have firmly believed, knowing from whom you learned it and how from childhood you have been acquainted with the sacred writings, which are able to make you wise for salvation through faith in Christ Jesus" (2 Tim. 3:14–15). Paul's appeal is for stability, for continuance in the Scriptures, on the grounds that Timothy has experienced already their trustworthy truth in his own life and family as well as through close observation of Paul's own life and ministry (2 Tim. 3:10–14).

Paul's main argument, though, builds on the double purpose—or what we could perhaps label as the job description—of the Scriptures. First, according to 2 Timothy 3:15, the Scriptures are able to make us wise to come to Christ by faith to find salvation. As the Bible story unfolds, God is progressively revealing himself through the Scriptures until, ultimately, he comes in person into our world. As we meet Jesus in the pages of the Gospels, we see the radiance of God's glory and the exact representation of his person (Heb. 1:3). This is what compels us to repent of our sin, accept his merciful forgiveness, and lay our lives before him as our Savior, Lord, and God.

The second purpose appears in the following verses: "All Scripture is breathed out by God and profitable for teaching, for reproof, for correction, and for training in righteousness, that the man of God may be complete, equipped for every good work" (2 Tim. 3:16–17). Because all Scripture is breathed out by God, it is the articulation in words of his mind and purposes. Because of *that*, all Scripture is profitable to teach what is right and to correct what is wrong. And this is necessary so that the man of God (a technical term for the pastor-teacher like Timothy) may be equipped for the task in all its aspects. The term "equipped" means that everything necessary has been provided to get the job done. Scripture is the pastor-teacher's totally sufficient resource for ministry because what Scripture says, God says.

Paul's solemn charge is, therefore, brief and to the point: "I charge you in the presence of God and of Christ Jesus, who is to judge the living and the dead, and by his appearing and his kingdom: preach the word; be ready in season and out of season; reprove, rebuke, and exhort, with complete patience and teaching" (2 Tim. 4:1–2). Whether or not it seems to be "in season," the word is always to be preached in order to do its work of reproving and rebuking so as to build up and strengthen the people of God. The need is urgent, then and now, because false teaching is constantly multiplying and spiritually destructive. But Timothy is not instructed to seek out or discover some new message. He is to keep faithful to the revelation already given; he is to preach the word, the word breathed out by God himself, whatever the personal cost might be.

Paul concludes, "As for you, always be sober-minded, endure suffering, do the work of an evangelist, fulfill your ministry" (2 Tim. 4:5). Paul warns Timothy not to allow any pressures, whether external opposition or internal uncertainty and divisions, to divert him from this primary calling. The apostle's confidence is entirely in the power of the preaching of the word of God to accomplish the work of God, both in the church and in the world. Only that confidence will keep the contemporary preacher unashamedly at this good work, whatever the responses. When God's word is faithfully preached, God's voice is authentically heard. Preaching matters because the God of the Bible is a speaking God, the only one.

2. Preaching Matters Because Christ Himself Is Its Supreme Focus

For this second principle, we turn again to the apostle Paul, this time writing to the church at Colossae. Again, the context is important. The Colossian Christians seem to have become diverted from seeing Christ as the full and sufficient revelation of God. Instead, they imagined that they could somehow add spiritual value by their own efforts. Paul's message is that in Christ the whole fullness of deity dwells bodily, and they have this fullness in union with Christ. Ascetic practices, religious rules and regulations, or speculative theological discussions can add nothing. In fact, to try to add to Christ is actually to subtract from him. Paul writes,

> Now I rejoice in my sufferings for your sake, and in my flesh I am
> filling up what is lacking in Christ's afflictions for the sake of his body,
> that is, the church, of which I became a minister according to the
> stewardship from God that was given to me for you, to make the word

of God fully known, the mystery hidden for ages and generations but now revealed to his saints. To them God chose to make known how great among the Gentiles are the riches of the glory of this mystery, which is Christ in you, the hope of glory. Him we proclaim, warning everyone and teaching everyone with all wisdom, that we may present everyone mature in Christ. For this I toil, struggling with all his energy that he powerfully works within me. (Col. 1:24–29)

Paul describes his God-given ministry as "to make the word of God fully known" (Col. 1:25). This means not so much teaching the whole Bible, Genesis to Revelation as it were, though that in itself is a laudable aim. Paul's point is that the fullness of God's word is Christ. What was hidden for ages has now been revealed. It has become an open secret, in which the riches of God's glory are disclosed. It has both a present experiential ingredient, "Christ in you" here and now, and also a wonderful future completion or fulfillment in "the hope of glory" (1:27). Christ is the summit and fullness of all God's revelation through his word, and so Paul's emphasis is unmissable. His is a ministry of proclamation, and the focus and substance of all his preaching is the open secret of God's mystery, which is Christ. *Him* we proclaim! That is why preaching matters so much—because Christ is its supreme focus.

Equally clear is Paul's teaching about the goal to which his preaching is directed. We proclaim Christ so that we may present everyone "mature," which means complete, "in Christ" (Col. 1:28). As the full truth about who Christ is and what he has accomplished is proclaimed through all the Scriptures, God's people are both warned of error and taught the truth. We are warned not to think that we will find the fullness of God's grace anywhere else than in Jesus Christ. It is only through the Scriptures, taught by the Holy Spirit, that we grow more and more into the image and likeness of our great Savior and Redeemer.

Paul takes it a step further when he writes to the Corinthians that "Jews demand signs and Greeks seek wisdom, but we preach Christ crucified, a stumbling block to Jews and folly to Gentiles, but to those who are called, both Jews and Greeks, Christ the power of God and the wisdom of God" (1 Cor. 1:22–24). Christ is the supreme focus of all biblical preaching, and the ongoing task of every expositor is to proclaim Christ crucified. We do not proclaim Christianity, either as a series of doctrinal propositions or a set of ethical instructions. Though both are biblical, they are not the center. We do not proclaim speculative theories of spirituality. We proclaim Christ. We do not proclaim health, happiness, and prosperity. We proclaim Christ—and him crucified.

All this is hard work. "For this I toil, struggling" is Paul's own testimony (Col. 1:29). In Greek literature, the verbs Paul uses appear in contexts that speak of hard, back-breaking manual labor, as well as in contexts that describe two athletes pitting their strength against each other in the wrestling arena, making every effort to overcome their opponent. Preaching takes everything we have—intellectually, emotionally, relationally. And if that was all Paul said, most of us would give up before we started. But wonderfully, he continues: "with all his energy that he powerfully works within me" (Col. 1:29). This energy is supernatural, Spirit-given, enabling the Bible preacher to keep working, wrestling, struggling, and persevering—first in the study and then in the pulpit. We want to proclaim "Jesus Christ and him crucified" (1 Cor. 2:2).

3. Preaching Matters Because Everyone Everywhere Needs to Hear

In Romans 10, Paul shares his heart for the conversion of unbelieving Israel. All through the letter the distinction between Jews and Gentiles has been operative, but their common need of God's rescuing grace in Christ becomes the increasingly dominant concern and focus. Paul states that in Christ "there is no distinction between Jew and Greek;

for the same Lord is Lord of all, bestowing his riches on all who call on him. For everyone who calls on the name of the Lord will be saved" (Rom. 10:12–13). He continues,

> How then will they call on him in whom they have not believed? And how are they to believe in him of whom they have not heard? And how are they to hear without someone preaching? And how are they to preach unless they are sent? As it is written, "How beautiful are the feet of those who preach the good news!" But they have not all obeyed the gospel. For Isaiah says, "Lord, who has believed what he has heard from us?" So faith comes from hearing, and hearing through the word of Christ. (Rom. 10:14–17)

The good news of salvation in and through the Lord Jesus Christ is a message the whole world needs to hear, and Paul's unpacking of the process by which that can happen puts preaching at its heart. Faith is produced through hearing the word of Christ, which requires a messenger to proclaim the gospel. This is the message that Christ himself first proclaimed and then commissioned his disciples to take to the ends of the earth (Matt. 28:19–20). That commission has never been rescinded, so preaching is supremely strategic. As Christ's saving work is made available to all, our privilege is to play a tiny part in building God's universal kingdom, which dwarfs man's greatest skyscrapers and which will last for eternity.

As John Stott puts it,

> There could be no hearers without heralds. . . . The essence of Paul's argument is seen if we put his six verbs in the opposite order: Christ sends heralds; heralds preach; people hear; hearers believe; believers call; and those who call are saved. And the relentless logic of Paul's case . . . is felt most forcibly when the stages are stated negatively and each is seen to be essential to the next. Thus, unless some people are

commissioned for the task, there will be no gospel preachers; unless the gospel is preached, sinners will not hear Christ's message and voice; unless they hear him, they will not believe the truths of his death and resurrection; unless they believe these truths they will not call on him; and unless they call on his name, they will not be saved.[2]

Preaching matters because it is God's appointed means by which the word of Christ is heard, the word that generates life-giving faith. We are not at liberty either to alter one letter of the content of God's messages or to dispense with God's method for its spread. Only in the sixty-six books of the canonical Scriptures can we be certain that we have the authentic word of the living God. Anything else will always be speculative. However powerful or engaging such a presentation may appear to be, if it is not God's word, it will not endure forever. There will always be demands for anything and everything else—miraculous signs, words of human wisdom, impressive communicators, powerful charisma. But we are to preach the word, to proclaim Christ. And that is what we must continue to do because such preaching reveals the heart's destiny. Response to God's word is the touchstone issue, both now and for eternity. That is why preaching matters and always will.

---

2 John R. W. Stott, *The Message of Romans*, The Bible Speaks Today (Leicester, UK: Inter-Varsity Press, 1994), 286–87.

2

What Is Expository Preaching?

MY AIM IN THESE opening chapters is to establish some vital, basic principles so that we have solid foundations in place to build on and develop our practical skills. Sometimes this means taking time carefully to define the terms we are using, and the word *expository* is an important case in point. Most preachers who use the Bible in their preaching would claim to be expository because something of biblical truth is included in what they say. That is all well and good. It is certainly preferable to preaching that is based on the preacher's bright ideas, but I want to use the term with a more specific and focused definition. An illustration may help us.

Let's think about our preaching using the analogy of a car. Here's the question: where is the Bible in the car? The illustration can equally be applied to your church or your own personal life, but we'll stick with our preaching as the focus.

For some preachers the Bible is out of sight in the trunk, hidden away and largely forgotten. As in many car trunks, the Bible in this illustration sits among a number of items that have been discarded and ignored. Preaching like this is governed by the preacher's own thoughts and opinions, discussion of current political and cultural issues, or just a series of agenda items for the management of the church. But the preacher is firmly in the driver's seat.

For others, the Bible seems to be permanently in the back seat not exercising any discernible influence on the preaching but perhaps once in a while providing an illuminating or provocative comment. Backseat drivers can cause considerable irritation to the driver, and for some the Bible has an inhibiting, restrictive effect. It belongs to a generation and a set of values long past so that it is best used only occasionally, if and when it chances to be relevant. This keeps the preacher still in the driver's seat.

Perhaps the most popular place for the Bible, however, is in the passenger seat, where it can certainly perform some useful functions. The Bible is viewed rather like a conversation companion on the journey, a sort of celestial satellite navigational system to help us travel in the right direction, a useful map reader to keep us on track. Such preaching uses the Bible to clarify or illustrate what the preacher wants to say, especially trying to make it relevant to today. But here, too, the preacher remains in the driver's seat.

The Principles of Expository Preaching

There is, of course, another place for the Bible in the car: firmly in the driver's seat. This is the defining mark of expository preaching.

Expository Preaching Is Driven by the Bible

The Bible determines the content of expository preaching because it takes the Bible seriously. The text of Scripture governs and directs all that the preacher says. Since we glorify the speaking God not only by listening to what he says but also by ensuring that his living and enduring word is our supreme authority in what we believe and how we live, that word must necessarily be at the center of our preaching.

Critics sometimes claim that this is equivalent to worshiping the Bible, displacing Christ from his proper headship in his church, or inhibiting the work of the Spirit. But how does Christ mediate his authority among his people? He rules by his word through the ministry of the Holy Spirit, opening the minds and hearts of God's people to its truth. So as the word is in the driver's seat, Christ—whose word it is—instructs and guides his people by his Spirit.

This is the testimony of the Lord Jesus himself in John 6:63: "It is the Spirit who gives life; the flesh is no help at all. The words that I have spoken to you are spirit and life." Later he promises the apostles that "when the Spirit of truth comes, he will guide you into all the truth, for he will not speak on his own authority, but whatever he hears he will speak. . . . He will glorify me, for he will take what is mine and declare it to you" (John 16:13–14). It is through the apostolic witness in the New Testament Scriptures that we hear Christ's voice. We do not worship the Bible, but it is the divinely appointed means by which we come to worship the true Christ—as revealed in the Scriptures—and not a figment of our own imagination.

Consider the alternative. If the word of God is not driving our preaching and teaching, then something or someone else will be. There are plenty of rival candidates. It may be the preacher's wisdom or originality, a charismatic personality, popular opinion in the congregation, or the social and political agendas of our current culture. But when we realize how unstable, transient, and subjective each of these will prove to be, the necessity of expository preaching becomes even more obvious. The apostle Paul warned the Ephesians that congregations are easily "tossed to and fro by the waves and carried about by every wind of doctrine" (Eph. 4:14). In contrast, when the Bible is in the driver's seat, the voice of God is heard, even through the imperfect human channel.

Of course, the Bible is a blending of the human and divine. The biblical books were given to us through the words of the original writers at specific points in space and time. The writers necessarily have different styles and write both from and to different historical and cultural contexts. Yet because the Scriptures are divinely inspired—"breathed out by God" (2 Tim. 3:16)—they have eternal significance and validity.

God did not give us a book of rules or a set of theological propositions. He spoke to and through real people in real life situations so that
the human ingredients are seamlessly woven together with the divine. To
grasp the Bible's unchanging divine message, we have to put ourselves in
the shoes of the original hearers or readers in their particular contexts.
When we see what the text meant to them, we soon realize that our
external cultural differences do not affect the Bible's continuing authority. Although all Scripture is culturally positioned, this fact does not
reduce its validity and relevance since its divine author is unchanging
and eternal. Its revelatory truth is not culturally conditioned.

Expository Preaching Recognizes That the Bible Determines the Structure and Scope of the Preaching

The Bible is to be in the driver's seat in determining not only the content of the preaching but also the shape and course of the exposition.
Beyond that, it should determine the very contours of our continuing
ministry. Starting with the premise that God must be, by definition, the
perfect communicator commits us not only to rigorous study of what
the biblical text says but also to recognition of the means by which its
significance is conveyed—such as the text's tone, literary characteristics,
genre, promises and meanings, encouragements and motivations. The
biblical text drives the *what* of preaching, but it drives the *how* and
the *why* as well.

It follows that expository preaching is normally practiced as the
systematic, consecutive treatment of successive passages through a
particular biblical book. It is preaching that works its way through
entire books or major sections of the Bible. This gives due recognition
to the way in which God has given us his word. Otherwise, one can
all too easily develop a butterfly mentality in the selection of preaching texts, hopping from topic to topic or extracting favorite passages
from their context. This pick-and-choose approach means that texts are
often treated in a stand-alone manner rather than understood within

their biblical contexts so that they may be related to the whole sweep of redemptive history. God's method, by contrast, is to produce whole books, each with its own unique purpose and serving a cumulative effect. Expository preaching uses the larger units to inform our understanding of a particular section and vice-versa so that our picture of the whole book begins to sharpen its focus.

I have sometimes tried to illustrate this by taking an open Bible in my hand and holding it, facing outwards, extending it toward my hearers. In doing so, I am indicating that the expositor's task is, with his finger firmly on the text, to guide his hearers through the passage. He does not want to stand in front of the Bible so that the congregation becomes preoccupied with him rather than God's word. That would effectively make him a barrier to the understanding of the message of the text. But neither should he hide behind the text, as though preaching were just an anonymous, faceless communication mechanism. Rather, in the act of preaching we have a further blending of the human and divine.

Expository Preaching Conveys God's Unchanging Truth through the Preacher's Individual Personality

No two preachers are alike because we all have different personalities. We should not try to be replicas of our favorite pulpit heroes, attempting to imitate their style, bearing, or gestures. We have to be ourselves as God has made us and is remaking us. Each preacher is uniquely shaped and equipped by God for the particular task and context he has for us to fulfill. So when someone comes to you with a well-intended compliment, "You know there's no one else who can preach like you," don't be flattered. It's just a statement of fact! There *is* no one else who will do it like you.

Phillips Brooks, an American pulpit giant of the nineteenth century, famously described preaching as "the bringing of truth through personality."[1] That is helpful because it guarantees a unique place for each

---

1 Phillips Brooks, *Lectures on Preaching: Delivered before the Divinity School of Yale College in January and February, 1877* (New York: E. P. Dutton & Company, 1907), 5.

individual preacher, yet always under the absolute control of the biblical text in the driver's seat. The common denominator for all preaching is the truth of God's word—truth that is communicated through our various personalities. Then it is the ministry of the Spirit to open the minds and hearts of people to accept, delight in, obey, and practice that truth.

We remind ourselves that "all Scripture is breathed out by God and profitable for teaching, for reproof, for correction, and for training in righteousness, that the man of God may be complete, equipped for every good work" (2 Tim. 3:16–17). The expository preacher recognizes that the authority for what he says does not lie within himself, nor in his learning, experience, presentation skills, or engaging style. None of these is to be scorned, but they could each be used equally to present error as to teach the truth. Everything depends on the content of the preaching.

The tendency for the preacher to impose his ideas on the text—we might call it "impository" preaching—is certainly alive and active in churches today. And sometimes it is hard for people to discern the difference, especially if the preacher has a dynamic personality. "Wasn't it amazing what he got out of that text?" people sometimes say, whereas the reality was perhaps, "Wasn't it amazing what he managed to smuggle into it?" No, the expository preacher is a person under authority—the authority of the divinely inspired, eternally significant, and valid word of God in all of the canonical Scriptures. Moreover, in proclaiming this message, his confidence is entirely centered on the enabling ministry of the Holy Spirit.

Summary

The Spirit of God takes the word of God to accomplish the work of God. Expository preaching does not have to be original, clever, or entertaining. It has to be faithful and obedient. The preacher sits under God's word in study and preparation, marinating his soul in its unchanging truth, and then he proclaims its intended meaning and significance through his individual personality.

Expository preaching is not a matter of trying to do something with an ancient or alien text; rather it is the text that does something in both the preacher and hearers. Driven by the Bible in its content, structure, and scope, expository preaching does not have to create relevance because nothing could be more relevant than the living and enduring word of the one true and living God.

Applying the Principles

In a culture where we are used to looking for a quick and easy fix to our problems, the huge volume of preached material available on the internet is both a challenge and temptation. Have you ever thought to yourself that there are lots of sermon websites with far better materials than you could produce? So why not download a quality offering, tweak it a little, and add an illustration or two to make it your own? It could be very tempting, but it will never make you an expositor.

If a preacher is not spending time directly meeting with God in his word, that word is not dwelling in him richly (Col. 3:16). Its unique place has been usurped by another preacher's work. The result is not a heart-to-heart proclamation of biblical truth that has been received, internalized, and preached. Rather, the result is a ministry of performance, like an actor speaking someone else's script. The sermon has become more important to us than the Scriptures. The danger is that the approval of the hearers will subtly start to matter more than the approval of God.

The Expository Preacher Seeks to Be the Mouth by Which God Speaks

This is an awesome and sobering concept, but it is well developed in a memorable quotation from John Calvin, commenting on Paul's phrase "able to teach" (1 Tim. 3:2). He comments,

> Paul does not mean that one should just make a parade here or that a man should show off so that everyone applauds him and says "Oh! well-spoken! Oh! what a breadth of learning! Oh! what a subtle mind!"

All that is beside the point. . . . When a man has climbed up into the
pulpit . . . it is so that God may speak to us by the mouth of a man.[2]

The awareness that the preacher is the mouth by which God speaks
produces a sense of holy privilege and solemn responsibility that will
keep us humble, hardworking, and dependent expositors of God's
word. This is needed not least because those who preach are particularly
prone to temptations to indulge the sinful nature. On the one hand,
when God is pleased to use our words and sermons, we may persuade
ourselves that we are really rather special. On the other hand, we will
be tempted to give way to discouragement and despair when nothing
appears to be happening. These opposite effects seem to have a common
root—namely, that the preacher has become too large in the equation
and God has become too small.

The purpose of preaching is not to build the reputation of the preacher,
nor even to grow the scope and influence of the ministry through the
church. Instead, it is that the voice of God may be heard "by the mouth
of a man"—the proclamation of living truth by living messengers.

There is a passage in 1 Corinthians that preachers would do well to
embrace. In this trendy, glitzy, cosmopolitan city, the church was being
overly influenced by its surrounding culture. A melting pot of ethnic
backgrounds and lifestyles, Corinth was an eclectic mix of all the latest
ideas and fashions. Apparently, some church members were increasingly dissatisfied with the apostle Paul, who was not nearly impressive
enough for a cutting-edge church that was so pleased with itself. There
were squabbles between different church factions that lined up behind
their favorite leaders. So Paul writes,

What then is Apollos? What is Paul? Servants through whom you
believed, as the Lord assigned to each. I planted, Apollos watered, but

2 Quoted in T. H. L. Parker, *Calvin's Preaching* (Edinburgh: T&T Clark, 1992), 24.

God gave the growth. So neither he who plants nor he who waters is anything, but only God who gives the growth. He who plants and he who waters are one, and each will receive his wages according to his labor. For we are God's fellow workers. (1 Cor. 3:5–9)

Paul's point is that preachers and leaders are by definition servants. They are selected and equipped by the Lord to be the human mouths through which he speaks. As with Apollos and Paul, the tasks may be different, but the terms of employment are the same. Neither preacher is responsible to produce spiritual life and development—that is God's prerogative alone, which means that any sort of rivalry or competition is irrelevant and destructive.

We need that conviction to be strongly rooted in us, especially in an age like ours that is very much like that in Corinth. Celebrity culture increasingly seduces the church. Young preachers often try to emulate their pulpit heroes. The emphasis can subtly shift from faithfulness, known only to God, to success as judged by human standards. Instead, we must seek to be servants who are faithful mouthpieces of God's word.

The Expository Preacher Puts His Confidence in the Message God Has Given

Later, in 1 Corinthians 4, Paul gives us further descriptions of those he has already called "God's fellow workers" (1 Cor. 3:9). He writes, "This is how one should regard us, as servants of Christ and stewards of the mysteries of God" (1 Cor. 4:1).

These phrases emphasize the sense that the preacher is ultimately responsible to the Lord alone. The judgment of Paul's fellow Christians in Corinth carried little weight with him because, as he says, "It is the Lord who judges me" (1 Cor. 4:4). That is the only assessment that matters in the end. For Paul, human judgment of his ministry is discounted, not because he is arrogant but because human judges often use the wrong criteria or pronounce judgment at the wrong time (see 1 Cor. 4:3–5).

Paul's confidence is not at all in the messenger, however gifted; much less is it in the assessments of others. Rather, Paul's confidence lies in the message because God is its author. That is why the Bible is in the driver's seat; it alone is God's living and enduring word. The expository preacher is confident in the living word because it is the living God who has given it. Paul wanted the Corinthians to learn "not to go beyond what is written, that none of you may be puffed up in favor of one against another. For who sees anything different in you? What do you have that you did not receive? If then you received it, why do you boast as if you did not receive it?" (1 Cor. 4:6–7).

The Expository Preacher Is Content to Be a Servant of Christ

Having heard Paul repeatedly describe the preacher as a servant, we need also to listen to the Lord Jesus himself deal with a dispute among the disciples as to which of them was to be regarded as the greatest. The irony of the context is that this conversation occurs on the last night of Jesus's earthly ministry immediately before his betrayal. Addressing his disciples, Jesus says, "The kings of the Gentiles exercise lordship over them, and those in authority over them are called benefactors. But not so with you. Rather, let the greatest among you become as the youngest, and the leader as one who serves. . . . I am among you as the one who serves" (Luke 22:25–27).

Jesus rebukes the disciples for having a worldly mindset, an attitude that defines success as controlling and dominating others. But greatness in the kingdom of God is measured by the yardstick of humble service, which Jesus is about to exemplify to its ultimate degree as he goes to the cross to give himself for the salvation of his people. That pattern of humble service is to be the lifestyle of all who proclaim his word in every place and generation.

It has been my observation throughout my years of Christian service that no minister or preacher can be truly useful to God's eternal purposes until he has been significantly and deeply humbled. Whatever gifts or talents may have been granted by God, they are of little ultimate value unless they are united to a heart submitted to the lordship of Christ. We need to give up our small ambitions to be someone or do something great for God. Instead, we must make it a lifelong practice to ask, "Lord, what will you have me do?" As servants, we have to be content to fill the smallest place if that is how we can best bring glory to God.

God has a myriad of ways to bring us to the end of our own resources so that we come ultimately to our only true position of strength: total dependence on him. Having learned this lesson in the hard school of experience, Peter warns us, "'God opposes the proud but gives grace to the humble.' Humble yourselves, therefore, under the mighty hand of God so that at the proper time he may exalt you" (1 Pet. 5:5–6). The expository preacher is someone on whose heart that lesson of spiritual usefulness is deeply ingrained—a mouthpiece for God through his word, confident in the message he has given and content to be nothing more than a servant of the Lord Jesus.

3

Are There Biblical Patterns?

GOD IS THE MASTER COMMUNICATOR. He made us in his image—with the ability to think and to articulate our thoughts in words—so that we can enter into communication with him, the speaking God, through the Bible and in prayer. That conversation provides the building blocks of relationship. We often rightly concentrate on the content of what God says—indeed, that is essential. But equally, we need to focus on *how* God is saying it, especially if we are to faithfully carry on his conversation initiative in our preaching. There are biblical patterns by which God has made himself known that provide blueprints for us to follow.

The Pattern Unfolds throughout the Old Testament

On the first page of the Bible, we find that God is speaking. His creative power is operative through what he says: " 'Let there be light,' and there was light" (Gen. 1:3). His words not only express his will but are also the agency by which his will is carried out. At God's spoken word, the whole created order is brought into existence. Not surprisingly, when humankind is created, God speaks to Adam and Eve both before the fall and afterward. This, then, becomes the pattern. What God does is explained by what God says.

God reveals himself through his actions and his words, just as we do in our human relationships since we are made in his image. He speaks to describe what he has done, what he is doing, or what he will do. This combination of words and actions reveals his character and his will. As a student, I remember hearing J. I. Packer express this in a single yet memorable formula:

Revelation = Event + Explanation

God intervenes. He does things in our real world of time and space that he has created. But this is no dumb show. He isn't playing a miming game in which we have to guess the significance. God explains. This is the pattern that preachers must follow if we are to be his authentic messengers. The following examples, from some key episodes in the Old Testament, help us see these patterns working out.

Abraham's unique relationship with God begins with divine intervention in his life:

> Now the LORD said to Abram, "Go from your country and your kindred and your father's house to the land that I will show you. And I will make of you a great nation, and I will bless you and make your name great, so that you will be a blessing. I will bless those who bless you, and him who dishonors you I will curse, and in you all the families of the earth shall be blessed." So Abram went, as the LORD had told him. (Gen. 12:1–4)

The command to leave (a major event in Abram's life) is supported by the promises of covenant blessing (God's explanation), which together generate his response of obedience. Alongside the event-and-explanation pattern, there is a parallel pattern of promise and faith. Abram obeys the divine command because he believes the divine promises, and this covenantal relationship constitutes the paradigm for the development of the Old Testament narrative. When God speaks to reveal his purposes, those who respond in faith and obedience enter into a relationship with their Creator, which is deepened and developed as they respond to his word. The story of Abraham is one of continuing promises and purposes received by faith, fulfilled by God's own actions, and explained by God's own words.

Following this pattern, God makes promises to Isaac and Jacob (Gen. 26:3–5, 24; 28:13–15). The nation of Israel is born and constituted as God's own people, redeemed through the Passover sacrifice and from their slavery in Egypt. But it is at Mount Sinai that they personally meet their rescuer. The pattern is repeated as they are gathered at the foot of the mountain to receive God's instructions in the commandments and laws of the covenant: "And God spoke all these words, saying . . ." (Ex. 20:1). The words God spoke, incorporating both command and promise, explain what the exodus events meant for them as God's people and instructed them how to live in the blessing of relationship with him.

Forty years later, with Israel on the edge of the promised land, God addresses them through Moses in the speeches that form the book of Deuteronomy. What marks out Israel as distinct from the other nations is that they are gathered together to hear God's word of instruction and explanation as he unfolds the events by which he has revealed himself. The same is true during the conquest of Canaan: "[Joshua] read all the words of the law, the blessing and the curse, according to all that is written in the Book of the Law. There was not a word of all that Moses commanded that Joshua did not read before all the assembly of Israel" (Josh. 8:34–35). The rehearsal of the events and the explanation of why God was giving them the land reveal how they are to live in the land in light of God's holiness and power.

The same pattern exists at the start of the monarchy in Samuel's day: "So Samuel told all the words of the Lord to the people who were asking for a king from him" (1 Sam. 8:10). These words explain what their request entails, along with the potential abuses, tyranny, and corruption

God foresaw. Much later, when the remnant returns from the exile in Babylon, the same pattern prevails under Ezra and Nehemiah: "They read from the book, from the Law of God, clearly, and they gave the sense, so that the people understood the reading" (Neh. 8:8). The events and actions of God in both the exile and the restoration are explained to the people by reference to the revelation already given. As God's word is heard and related to their circumstances, they receive divine revelation about how they are to respond.

The covenant people of God are formed under, governed by, and sustained through the word of the speaking God. Moreover, throughout Israel's history, God raised up prophets to be the preachers of his covenant promises. They recall God's past interventions, explain his present actions, and disclose his future purposes, calling his people to respond in faith and obedience to the unique revelation they receive.

The Pattern Comes to Its Climax and Fulfillment in Jesus Christ

This point is established by the writer of the letter to the Hebrews, who underlines that both the Old and New Testaments are one coherent revelation with Christ as the apex and focus: "Long ago, at many times and in many ways, God spoke to our fathers by the prophets, but in these last days he has spoken to us by his Son, whom he appointed the heir of all things, through whom also he created the world" (Heb. 1:1–2).

In the incarnation of Jesus, the pattern reaches its peak since he is the living Word, who constantly enacts the Father's will and consistently speaks the Father's word of truth. The fact that Jesus has come as a proclaimer of God's truth and revealer of his nature is stressed from the beginning of his ministry. Indeed, at the height of his early popularity in Galilee when everyone wanted him to heal, Jesus said to his disciples, "Let us go on to the next towns, that I may preach there also, for that is why I came out" (Mark 1:38). The verb translated "preach" means to communicate with authority, to proclaim, to herald. Do you see how true this is to the established pattern? What God does is explained by what God says. And about Jesus he says, "This is my beloved Son, with whom I am well pleased; listen to him" (Matt. 17:5).

Perhaps the clearest and most obvious Gospel context in which we can grasp the pattern is Luke's account of Jesus visiting the synagogue in Nazareth at the beginning of his public ministry:

> The scroll of the prophet Isaiah was given to him. He unrolled the scroll and found the place where it was written,
>
> > "The Spirit of the Lord is upon me,
> >> because he has anointed me
> >> to proclaim good news to the poor.
> > He has sent me to proclaim liberty to the captives
> >> and recovering of sight to the blind,
> >> to set at liberty those who are oppressed,
> > to proclaim the year of the Lord's favor."
>
> And he rolled up the scroll and gave it back to the attendant and sat down. And the eyes of all in the synagogue were fixed on him. And he began to say to them, "Today this Scripture has been fulfilled in your hearing." (Luke 4:17–21)

Clearly, this is a direct claim to be the anointed one, the Christ. The verb repeated three times, "to proclaim," provides the purpose for his coming into the world. Good news, liberty, sight, favor—all these and more are the evidence or explanation of the event. His mighty works of miraculous power and his impeccable godly character require the explanation provided by his matchless teaching. But his actions and his explanation of them are the means by which his true identity is revealed.

Thus, when Jesus commissions his disciples at the end of his time on earth, it is not surprising that the pattern for the church is identical: "All authority in heaven and on earth has been given to me. Go therefore and make disciples of all nations, baptizing them . . . , teaching them to observe all that I have commanded you" (Matt. 28:18–20). That is the apostolic calling, and it became the apostolic practice. It shows that the revelation of God, through his actions and his words of explanation, must be the central ingredient of their preaching—and ours.

Understanding what God teaches us about his character and purposes should govern and shape our lives in his world. That is what the Bible is for. The Bible is God's book about God before it is his book about us. We look first, in every passage of Scripture, for God's activity and then for his explanation, which will enable us to apply the text to our contemporary context. Rather than putting ourselves and our concerns at the center of our preaching, we need to ask what God is teaching us about himself: what he has done, what he is saying, and what our response must be.

Further Examples

1 Corinthians 15:3. In this verse, Paul writes, "Christ died for our sins in accordance with the Scriptures." The revelatory content is dependent on an event ("Christ died"), a reality in space-time history. But the verse also requires the explanation of its purpose ("for our sins"), without which the event could appear either as a pointless act of self-martyrdom or a huge mistake. Both ingredients are needed for the revelation of the cross to be made clear.

Mark 1:9–11. Mark records the baptism of Jesus in which the heavens open and the Spirit descends on him like a dove. But the event requires explanation if its significance is to be clear. This comes directly from heaven: "You are my beloved Son; with you I am well pleased" (Mark 1:11). The declaration joins two

Old Testament quotations that speak about "my Son" who is God's conquering King (see Ps. 2:6–9) and "my servant" in whom the Lord "delights" (Isa. 42:1). This provides the divine explanation that Isaiah's prophecy is now at last being fulfilled in Jesus.

Luke 5:17–26. This narrative presents the healing of a paralyzed man, an event with two parts. The first part is visible—the paralytic walks. The second part is invisible—his sins are forgiven. The event requires an explanation and an answer to the question, "Who can forgive sins but God alone?" (Luke 5:21). The inference is clear. What is seen, the healing, is the proof of the divine power that can also accomplish what is not seen, the forgiveness of sins. And both can only be explained by the revelation of the healer, the "Son of Man" (Luke 5:24), to whom is given everlasting power and dominion (see Dan. 7:13–14).

The Pattern Is Passed On and Shapes the Apostolic Preaching

We see the first biblical example of a Christian sermon when the apostle Peter preaches on the day of Pentecost after the Holy Spirit was given to the believers in Acts 2:1–41. Peter's message to a large audience gathered in Jerusalem has three distinct components.

First, beginning with the immediate event—the wind, the tongues of fire, and speaking in other tongues (Acts 2:2-4) "telling . . . the mighty works of God" (Acts 2:11)—Peter explains the manifestation of the Spirit (Acts 2:16–21). This divine action is God's fulfillment of his promise in Joel 2:28–32, which ends with the key announcement that "everyone who calls upon the name of the Lord shall be saved" (Acts 2:21).

Second, Peter relates the explanation of the events, conveying their significance and purpose. He connects the promise of salvation in Joel to the life and death of Jesus of Nazareth. In Acts 2:22–36 he describes the events concerning Jesus—his mighty works, his betrayal and crucifixion, and his resurrection from the dead. This explanation is the major content of Peter's proclamation. With the emphasis on the resurrection, the event that proves all Christ's claims to be true, Peter explains its significance as the fulfillment of what God had said through David in Psalm 16. He then applies this and another Messianic quotation from Psalm 110 to Jesus. His sermon reaches its climax with the declaration, "Let all the house of Israel therefore know for certain that God has made him both Lord and Christ, this Jesus whom you crucified" (Acts 2:36).

Finally, when his hearers respond to the revelation with the question "What shall we do?" Peter calls them to repent and be baptized in the name of Jesus Christ for the forgiveness of sins and to receive the gift of the Holy Spirit (Acts 2:37–38). Thus, Peter recounts what God has done, relates it to what God has said and is saying, and then tells his hearers what they must do. The events and their explanation constitute the revelation to which they must respond.

Alongside Peter's Pentecost sermon, Acts 17:16–34 is a helpful text to examine, as it exemplifies Paul's approach to a non-Jewish audience. Arriving in Athens, the intellectual capital of the Greco-Roman world, Paul begins as usual by reasoning in the synagogue but accompanies this with daily marketplace evangelism among any willing to listen. Eventually, he is invited to address the Areopagus, the oldest and most revered tribunal in the city, to explain his beliefs before some of the most influential Athenian citizens.

He begins with what is immediately familiar to the personal experience of his hearers. Paul has seen in this religious city—full of idols, shrines, and temples—an altar "to the unknown god." But he takes them back to events much further away, at the dawn of history, of which his educated hearers are ignorant. In a context where his listeners do not know the Old Testament Scriptures, Paul doesn't start with a text, as in the synagogue. Nevertheless, without quoting a text, he uses the theology contained in the Scriptures to reveal what God has done. These biblical realities are then related directly to the mistakes and ignorance of the Athenians' religious practice.

Paul uses biblical revelation to deconstruct pagan idolatry. He exposes their spiritual ignorance by explaining the great realities of the true and living God. The true God does not live in temples because he created the world in which we live (Acts 17:24–25). He is not served by human hands that make offerings at his shrine, as though he needed these things, because he gives us life, breath, and everything we need to sustain us (Acts 17:25). He is not one among a variety of gods for different cultures because he made every nation from one man (Acts 17:26). He is not remote and unknowable. Instead, we are his offspring, and he wants us to be in relationship with him (Acts 17:27). In other words, Paul is declaring that the only true and living God is both the explanation and solution for everything they see and know. This is biblical deconstructionism, as Paul uses revelation to expose the fallacies of and undermine the plausibility of Athenian culture.

He then moves to the heart of his message by building on this revelation his hearers have just received, continuing to focus on God. God overlooked the times of ignorance, but now he commands all people everywhere to repent because he has given proof that he will judge the world by raising Jesus—the "man whom he has appointed"—from the dead (Acts 17:30–31). Paul challenges them to recognize that God has intervened in our world through this man and will intervene again when he comes to judge. Even to pagan Athens, Paul "was preaching Jesus and the resurrection." As always, the responses varied, from mockery to faith (Acts 17:32–34).

In each of these examples, the hearers are faced with gospel realities, described and explained, which are designed to make them question their presuppositions. God is proclaimed as powerful, yet good and gracious, the only source of salvation and freedom. The events of the crucifixion and resurrection of Christ are proclaimed and explained to prove that Jesus is the one true and living God, in human form, and that he is the only true source of forgiveness and freedom, justification and joy. The reality of the living God is revealed in all his rescuing power.

Further Examples

Acts 13:16–41. This passage provides the account of the apostle Paul's address to the synagogue congregation in Pisidian Antioch. Like Peter on the day of Pentecost, Paul speaks to Jewish people who knew the Old Testament Scriptures and respected their authority. He begins by recounting how God has acted through past events in Israel's history, culminating in the ministry of John the Baptist who introduced the promised Savior (Acts 13:17–25). The sermon then concentrates on the events concerning Jesus's death and resurrection (Acts 13:27–33), with references both to Old Testament prophecy and to the eyewitnesses of the risen Jesus.

The explanation of the events is woven throughout the historical narrative. God is the subject of all the verbs describing Israel's history. He is the hero of the nation's story. The focus is on his saving activity and gracious promises so that the link to Christ is clear. "Of this man's [David's] offspring God has brought to Israel a Savior, Jesus, as he promised" (Acts 13:23). Here is the culmination of God's salvation plan, not in terms of a national political deliverance for Israel but at the level of each individual believer's personal experience. He concludes, "Let it be known to you therefore, brothers, that through this man [Jesus] forgiveness of sins is proclaimed to you, and by him everyone who believes is freed from everything from which you could not be freed by the law of Moses" (Acts 13:38–39).

Paul challenges his hearers to accept the forgiveness and freedom, which could never be theirs through the law, that are now available through Christ alone.

Acts 17:1–4. Paul's missionary method in the cities he visited is highlighted in these verses. Arriving in Thessalonica he goes to the Jewish synagogue, as was his custom (Acts 17:1). The focus of his message is the events of Christ's suffering, death, and resurrection. Paul does this by "explaining and proving that it was necessary for the Christ to suffer" (Acts 17:3) and reasoning from the Scriptures (17:2)—whose authority the Jews already accepted. Some were persuaded of the truth of Paul's central affirmation: "This Jesus, whom I proclaim to you, is the Christ" (Acts 17:3). The retelling of the events and their explanation was designed to achieve that very response of faith.

It is striking that the same verbs occur in every subsequent context of the apostle's ministry—reasoning, proclaiming, persuading. In Berea, "the word of God was proclaimed" (Acts 17:13). In Athens, Paul "reasoned in the synagogue . . . and in the market place every day," "preaching Jesus and the resurrection" (Acts 17:17–18). In Corinth, he "reasoned . . . and tried to persuade" (18:4), "testifying . . . that the Christ was Jesus" (Acts 18:5). In Ephesus, Paul was "reasoning and persuading them about the kingdom of God" (Acts 19:8), "reasoning daily . . . so that all the residents . . . heard the word of the Lord" (19:9–10).

It is possible, of course, to teach the contents and events of the Bible much like an academic exercise, conveying its information as historical realities but to go no further or deeper. That was not Paul's approach. Whether in his evangelism or his pastoral nurture of the churches, his preaching was always designed to

> bring about change in his hearers, an alignment of their values and behavior with what God requires. Responding to God's truth revealed in Christ by repentance and faith is not only the way *to begin* the Christian life but also the way *to continue*.

Timothy Keller has written cogently,

Paul does not "change" the gospel, but only "adapts" it. And this is the very key to effective ministry. If we never adapt the gospel, we will be completely ineffective. Like Paul, we must deeply discern the particular beliefs, hopes, aspirations, fears, prejudices, and wisdom of others or our gospel communication will seriously miss the mark. But if we change or lose the basics of the gospel, we will also be completely ineffective. Like Paul, we must not shrink from declaring that there is only one true God, that every single person (no matter how nice and good) is sinfully trying to be his or her own Lord and Savior, that Jesus was really divine and human, that he died in our place and was raised bodily from the dead. The basic truths and "events" are non-negotiable. To alter or omit any of them leads to the loss of distinctive Christianity.[1]

Every church needs to preach the gospel and proclaim the whole counsel of God consistently through explaining the content of the text and applying it to the hearers with a call for response. This is the biblical pattern given to us by God, which is never outdated and which is our responsibility to fulfill and pass on, from one generation to the next.

---

1   Timothy J. Keller, *Evangelism: Studies in the Book of Acts, Leaders' Guide* (New York: Redeemer Presbyterian Church, 2005), 121.

4

What Are the Contemporary Challenges?

TO BE A FAITHFUL and effective biblical preacher has never been an easy task. Over four hundred years ago, the English Puritan William Perkins wrote a book about preaching entitled *The Art of Prophesying*.[1] In it he laments the fact that few men of ability were seeking the calling of the ministry and that, of those who did, few deserved the name of messenger and interpreter. He traces this to the contempt in which the preacher was held because his task was to reveal sin and unmask hypocrisy. But it was also due, Perkins notes, to the difficulty of the work since speaking to people on behalf of God is truly an overwhelming and awesome responsibility.

Although we live in a different time and social context, Perkins's words are equally applicable today. Our challenges are many and come from a variety of different directions. But we need to be realistic about them, face the difficulties, and find God's way to deal with them, if we are to be faithful and effective in our own generation.

Facing the Challenges in Our Culture

Of course, culture is never monochrome. Our danger is that we tend to stereotype and oversimplify cultures that differ from our own, while

1 William Perkins, *The Art of Prophesying: And the Calling of the Ministry* (repr., Edinburgh, UK: Banner of Truth Trust, 2021).

failing to recognize the wide variety of attitudes and responses in the culture we know best. However, in many parts of the world, "preach" has become a negatively charged word. "Don't you preach at me!" is a common response to any sort of moral instruction or advice. Many moderns are incredulous: "What right do you have to tell me how to live my life?"

Inescapable Issues

We begin with a double credibility problem: what we say (an authoritative word from God) and how we convey it (preaching) both lack any positive resonance in contemporary, secularistic cultures. We start on the back foot, at least across the liberalized Western democracies. In other cultures, the religious teacher may still command some respect, but the forces of secular globalization will increasingly erode that advantage. For many, the traditional monologue church pulpit is the archetypal example of the control mechanisms and power ploys that are said to lie at the heart of all religions.

The current social and philosophical climate powerfully reinforces this reaction, and the internet spreads the culture of relativism everywhere. Truth, so-called, is the creation of the individual, influenced by peer groups and favorite social media sites. Consequently, there can be no moral absolutes. All people have the right to live their lives their own way, so long as it brings them happiness—the greatest goal—without doing harm to others.

This cultural ethos presents a challenge, therefore, to the method of authoritative proclamation. A church and perhaps a lecture hall are the only places remaining where it is customary to sit and listen to a monologue. Increasingly, educational methods from kindergarten to university are based on interactive discovery models that have made the up-front "chalk and talk" method of instruction outdated, redundant, and consigned to the dustbin of history. Should preaching equally be jettisoned? No, because the objection is more basic than a rejection of methodology. Fundamentally, it is a resistance to the authority of the content, to the word that is preached. The presuppositions in our culture run much deeper: "Why should we accept the Bible as anything more than a collection of human writings with varying degrees of weight or relevance? Surely, we have evolved beyond its antiquated notions, so we need not pay attention to those who preach its uncompromising assertions." If we cannot, do not, or will not respond to these issues, we will fail to make any significant connections with our culture. Attractive but fatal alternatives present themselves.

Dangerous Diversions

A typical response of the preacher who feels insecure in content or method is to go into overdrive. The weaker the content, the louder the shouting. The less persuasive the argument, or lack of it, the more melodramatic the presentation. It is as though the issues could be answered by increasing the volume or hyping-up the enthusiasm level. Or perhaps one just becomes increasingly authoritarian: "You'd better believe it because I'm saying it to you." Yet, such a response is totally counterproductive in the end. Alternatively, the insecure preacher may decide to go low profile so that he neither challenges anything nor suggests that change is necessary. Such preaching becomes a hodgepodge of pseudo-Christian ideas and secular political correctness so as not to offend anyone. Platitudes rule the sermon. Everything is comfortable and incredibly nice, with the result that the preacher has a quiet life and the church sinks into terminal decline.

Facing the Challenges in Our Churches

We must realize that the cultural challenges we face exist within the church as well. When the apostle Paul exhorted the Romans not to be "conformed to this world" (Rom. 12:2), he was recognizing that the prevailing views of the age in which we live will exert pressure on Christian people to compromise their distinctive beliefs and behavior.

Inescapable Issues

For many in our congregations, the cultural rejection of any ulti-mate authority—beyond that of one's own experience—drip feeds into their attitude toward Scripture and God's self-revelation. Every time someone says, "I like to think that God . . . ," they indicate that their ultimate value system is grounded in themselves. When preaching challenges long held presuppositions, listeners may react by questioning the preacher's interpretation. "After all, you can make the Bible mean anything," people will say. "That's just *your* interpretation!"

Another factor to consider is that many have had disappointing experiences of preaching so that the thought of it leads to boredom, disillusionment, and even despair. The Puritan poet John Milton in his poem "Lycidas" complains that "the hungry sheep look up, and are not fed,"[2] and in some contexts today that is still the case. God's sheep need good grazing and green pastures. They need the nourishment of the good word of God, though they are often unaware of it. In such situations where spiritual sustenance is lacking, even ten minutes of boring plati-tudes can seem like an eternity. Expectations of a life-giving encounter with the living God in his word do not feature on the Sunday agenda, and so the terminal decline of Christian faith and witness continues.

Sadly, there are congregations that do not want anything more than a cozy community get-together. They want the preaching to be pre-dictable and comfortable, reinforcing their existing understanding and outlook. In such a climate, therapy replaces theology, testimony edges out truth, and sometimes human imagination usurps biblical fact. Such a famine of God's word is bound to leave congregations undernourished and vulnerable. The symptoms are not hard to identify. It becomes increasingly difficult to persuade congregation members to commit to serving or even to regular attendance. Personal needs remain unmet, hearts inevitably harden, and members slipping out the back door far

---

2   John Milton, "Lycidas," line 125.

outweigh any newcomers coming in the front. As a result, the church's ministry focuses on the management of decline.

Dangerous Diversions

Such church challenges can cause the preacher to lose heart, to consider that the path of change will be too long and difficult to be realistic. The temptation is to allow the congregation's current attitude to dictate the preacher's responses. Furthermore, although congregation members may rarely confess that they have been helped by the preaching, they may have little hesitation in offering critique and disagreement. Because the preacher wants to be a person of peace, the tendency can be to avoid grasping any nettles and to downplay the need for repentance and change. Thus, nothing changes and no progress is made.

Alternatively, the preacher may retreat into the secure and protected environment of his personal interest and study so that the sermons become increasingly academic, theoretical, and complex in presentation. Then again, the preacher may decide that the lack of listener response or interest means that everything has to be scaled down to the most elementary level, and thus the preaching becomes progressively more simplistic and patronizing. Along these lines, someone once commented to me, "I rarely go to church because when I do I am always treated like a child." All of this is symptomatic of an unwillingness to recognize and deal with the practical obstacles that need to be overcome. But there is one further level of challenge we need to address.

Facing the Challenges in Ourselves

In the light of the challenges identified above, to feel inadequate for this great task is a good and healthy response. Outlining the demands of his apostolic ministry in 2 Corinthians 2:16, Paul asks, "Who is sufficient for these things?" But he answers his own question a few verses later, stating that "our sufficiency is from God, who has made us sufficient to be ministers of a new covenant" (2 Cor. 3:5–6). Knowing that he is not sufficient in himself, Paul puts his faith in God's sufficiency—which is quite different from the paralyzing lack of confidence felt by many preachers.

Inescapable Issues

A preacher's sense of inadequacy may center on feeling ill-equipped, either in one's understanding of the content and purpose of the biblical text or in one's understanding of the hearers and their needs. Theological training rarely prepares students to be competent preachers. Once a preacher begins ministry, helpful honest feedback or constructive critical analysis is difficult to come by. So the preacher may feel very alone, questioning the value of what he is trying to accomplish and soon deciding that perhaps preaching is not his gift. As a result, he may allocate it the minimum amount of time in his busy schedule and focus on other aspects of ministry.

Dangerous Diversions

Preachers face dangers in such circumstances. Perhaps the biggest is the temptation to transfer our dissatisfaction with our own preaching to a dissatisfaction with our sources of truth and power. What I mean is that we can begin to lose confidence in the word of God to do its work or in the power of the Spirit of God to change lives through the preaching. We need to be aware of the symptoms.

Lack of confidence in the power of Scripture will lead to poor work in the study, little in-depth focus on the text, and an increasing inclination to cut corners in preparation. If we lack confidence in the power of the Holy Spirit, it will lead to a lack of prayer since we will have little expectation that God can use our feeble efforts to accomplish his purposes in the lives of our hearers. A further symptom of a loss of confidence in the word and the Spirit is that we may tend to become ultra-defensive. We assume that anyone who criticizes our preaching—however well-intentioned—is an enemy of the gospel, which of course is far from true. This often leads to feelings of depression that generate a vicious circle: less time spent in preparation and prayer, resulting in preaching that is less engaging, resulting in less time spent in preparation and prayer, and on it goes. The church will begin to drift further toward the culture's estimate of preaching as outmoded and ineffective. There are fewer ears to hear, and the famine of God's word leaves the congregation malnourished, hungry, and exposed.

Because the contemporary challenges are so many and so varied, our current situation calls for us to be preachers who are single-minded in our devotion to the task. Of course, there are many other legitimate demands on a minister's time and energy, so much so that we sometimes resemble the circus performer who spins his plates on the ends of sticks, adding extras all the time and desperately doing his best to keep them all turning. But preaching requires dedication. A better analogy is that of the skilled surgeon. The operational skills of the work have been mastered, along with a fund of medical knowledge and a record of experience. But all this has to be applied differently from patient to patient. Every operation is unique and so is every sermon, which is the tool of the soul doctor at work. Surgeons did not pick up their abilities by browsing the internet for half an hour. Such expertise required dedication, discipline, hard work, and sacrifice. It is no different for the preacher.

Seven Strategies for Facing Our Challenges

As we face our contemporary challenges, let us think about seven strategies as principles for action that we need to internalize and develop.

1. Determine That Prayer Will Be Foundational

People often ask me where prayer fits in to a preacher's preparation and practice. The answer is that prayer fits at every stage, from the initial reading of the text to the preaching of the sermon, because it is the foundation of everything that happens. The whole process is an aspect of being in Christ, as we draw upon his resources and he graciously empowers us to do his will. Jesus said, "Whoever abides in me and I in him, he it is that bears much fruit, for apart from me you can do nothing" (John 15:5). Not just a little. Nothing! In prayer we open the door of our needs and desires to Christ's enabling power, so it must be at the heart of everything we do. This is how we can face all and any challenges as they become apparent. We must pray for ourselves, our hearers, and our church, but let's not forget to pray as well for our culture with its particular needs and lost-ness. We must speak to God about the lost world before we attempt to speak to the lost world about God.

2. Develop a Robust Doctrine of Scripture

As always, we need to know what we believe and why we believe it. We must be able to articulate and justify our commitment to the whole of Scripture as the living and enduring word of God, inspired, infallible, and inerrant. We need often to revisit the historic creeds and the Reformation confessions, using our denominational biblical affirmations as the solid foundations on which biblical ministry is to be built. For example, "The authority of the Holy Scripture, for which it ought to be believed, and obeyed, depends not upon the testimony of any man, or church; but wholly upon God (who is truth itself) the author thereof: and therefore it is to be received, because it is the Word of God."[3]

What preachers really believe about the status and authority of the Bible will be the single biggest influence on their preaching. Confidence in the authority and consequent power of the Scriptures will lead to a personal, humble submission to God's word in one's life and teaching. It will increase our determination to proclaim Christ to a lost world and to preach the whole counsel of God. That will enable us not to lose our spiritual priorities or to lapse into merely purvey-

---

3   Westminster Confession of Faith 1.4.

ing Christianized therapies, mechanized programs, or entertaining anecdotal pep talks.

3. Deepen Your Dependence on the Holy Spirit

If we did not believe that God's Spirit alone can give spiritual life and that only he can produce godly maturity, which of us would dare to preach? But what we believe foundationally has to be woven into the fabric of our lives and ministries. All the way through our preparation, we must be asking the Spirit for his illumination as we dialogue with him about the meaning of the text he has inspired and its application to life today.

We see a striking insight in Paul's words to Timothy: "Think over what I say, for the Lord will give you understanding in everything" (2 Tim. 2:7). Thinking is hard work. Indeed, the illustrations Paul uses in the preceding verses underline just how demanding the work of the ministry is. The pastor-teacher is a soldier facing hardships, an athlete exercising self-discipline, and a farmer demonstrating diligence and patience (2 Tim. 2:3–6). So we are to do the hard work of thinking over what God is saying, which will take time and effort. But what comes next? The text does *not* say, "And you will gradually be able to work out the meaning and application." That would be to ground our confidence in ourselves and our abilities. Paul's exhortation to "think over what I say" has a motivating connection: *for* the Lord gives the understanding. As we work, so does the Spirit in and through our endeavors to give the understanding.

We can have the highest academic grades, our bookshelves stacked with the greatest works of biblical scholarship, past and present—and these can certainly be of immense value—but faithful, effective preaching depends on asking the Lord to give understanding and submitting to his word. Eye-opening grace is not only essential but always available. As God's Spirit directs our preparation and empowers our proclamation, so *he* opens blinded minds, softens hardened hearts, and raises the spiritually dead to life. This is what he delights to do, so we must never confuse our task with his but deepen our fellowship with him and our dependence on him in our ministry.

4. Designate the Building Up of Your Hearers as Your Priority

Many of the practical problems in our churches and in our engagement with contemporary culture stem from a famine of clear, well-applied biblical exposition. Congregations that are not nurtured on a regular diet of biblical food will soon become anemic and run down. The biblical pattern is that the church is led by the preaching and teaching ministry of the word (see, e.g., Paul's charge to Timothy in 2 Tim. 4:1–5).

The apostolic pattern of ministry was affirmed very early in the church's life, when the apostles declared, "It is not right that we should give up preaching the word of God to serve tables" (Acts 6:2). Rather, they tell the whole church, "We will devote ourselves to prayer and to the ministry of the word" (Acts 6:4). The shepherd-teacher is called to dedicate his time, gifts, and energy to prayer, preparation, and the proclamation of God's truth as the means by which God's flock is fed and led. If we are going to meet the contemporary challenges in church life, we must prioritize this ministry above all the other claims on our time and energies. Seeing how churches change over a period of time through a regular, systematic, consecutive exposition of the Scriptures is a tremendous incentive to keep on keeping on with this essential service of love.

5. Don't Be Diverted into Celebrity Models of Ministry

Let's resolve before God to resist being drawn into competitive views of ministry. We live in a culture where image matters more than substance and where success, measured by popularity, can easily tempt us to sacrifice personal integrity. Typically, everyone wants to be recognized, approved, and even famous—if only for half an hour! We would be naïve to think that we are unaffected by such values. A celebrity-obsessed culture will look for preachers who become celebrities themselves, and we will be tempted to join them. As a student, I remember being warned that people will want to put you on a pedestal when you are a minister and that you will want to let them. But remember, too, that everything on a pedestal can come crashing down at any moment!

We need to resolve before God not to be seduced by human measurements of success in ministry, not to be envious of the greater gifts or opportunities of others so that we will not regard them as competitors. We must not be trapped into making a priority of our personal promotion within the structures of our church or denomination. That may be God's calling for some, but to set our hearts on it will almost certainly skew our ministry values and expose us to both jealousies and disappointments. We must not seek to build a personal empire out of our ministries. The apostle Paul is refreshingly straight about this when he warns the Corinthians not to line up behind their preferred human leaders and "be puffed up in favor of one against another" (1 Cor. 4:6). His questions are very searching: "For who sees anything different in you? What do you have that you did not receive? If then you received it, why do you boast as if you did not receive it?" (1 Cor. 4:7).

No one has all spiritual gifts! All of us are flawed and fragile jars of clay whom God has appointed to be bearers of the light of the gospel (2 Cor. 4:7). His is the power and the glory. To be competitive or envious of others is to demonstrate a Corinthian sort of immaturity. There are few outstandingly gifted preachers in any generation or location, and they are raised up by God to do an individual, distinctive work for him. We are neither to envy nor copy them. We thank God for them and can learn much from them, but we are not called to replicate them in style or personality. We must be ourselves, in Christ, as we do our best to present ourselves to God (not to others) as workers who have no need to be ashamed, rightly handling the word of truth (2 Tim. 2:15).

6. Dialogue with the World and Its Culture

One of the major ways to resist the eroding effects of the prevailing culture—both secular and religious—is to dialogue with its claims, to uncover its presuppositions, and to answer its objections. The most dangerous response is to withdraw, pull up the drawbridge, and concentrate on defending our castle. History shows that when that happens, evangelism withers and internal struggles multiply. A church turned inward will always tend to devour itself in a fruitless quest for perfection, creating internal enemies and endless controversy. There is, of course, an equivalent danger in which engaging with the world degenerates into becoming almost indistinguishable from it—unless everything is assessed by strongly held, nonnegotiable biblical convictions.

In addition to being aware of our culture's prevailing attitudes and assumptions, we need to examine our own presuppositions and be especially clear about why we believe what we believe. Although Christ's disciples are "not of the world" (John 17:16), they are still "in the world" (John 17:11), a tension that we experience daily and that runs throughout the Bible. Israel was to be distinct from the other nations, yet not isolated. Their privilege was to receive God's word of instruction (torah) and, by their obedience to it, be distinguished for their wisdom and understanding, serving as a light to the nations. Similarly, the church is called to be the salt of the earth and the light of the world (Matt. 5:13–14)—images of the church's penetration of the world's decay and darkness.

The biblical preacher must live in both the word and the world—or as Paul typically expressed it, "in Christ Jesus . . . at Philippi" (Phil. 1:1). We need to keep abreast with the prevailing worldviews, fashions, trends, and developments of our cultural environment, especially within the academic world that is educating the generation that will soon be reshaping popular culture. But while we need to be in constant dialogue with the world, the culture must never be in the driver's seat. That place is reserved for God's word, which will teach us what we need to know about the world and enable us to apply its truth to the particularities of our own day and location.

7. Develop Authenticity in Both Life and Teaching

The final strategy reminds us never to underestimate the powerful effect of the preacher's life to corroborate the trustworthiness of the message proclaimed. "Keep a close watch on yourself and on the teaching," Paul exhorts Timothy. "Persist in this, for by so doing you will save both yourself and your hearers" (1 Tim. 4:16). The Greek word for "hypocrite" originally referred to an actor, one who put on a mask to speak someone else's words and portray someone else's character. Preachers of God's word, in contrast, must practice what they preach. They must continuously submit their lives to the Lord's authority and meet his message in their own souls with faith and obedience. Our lives must embody what we preach if we are to build up others with any degree of integrity.

Nearly sixty years ago, the German theologian and preacher Helmut Thielicke published a book entitled *The Trouble with the Church*. He explored why the Reformation view of preaching as "the source and spring of Christian faith" was no longer current in Europe.[4] This question was central to his inquiry: Does the preacher really live "in the house of the dogmas he proclaims?"[5] His sad conclusion was that many a preacher no longer lived "in the house of his utterance."[6] If the preachers no longer believed—personally and passionately—the truth they preached, then the hearers would soon become unbelievers too. People know when preaching is from the heart, and they respond accordingly. They know when someone loves and cares for them, and they warm to the message delivered through such a messenger. We only really learn

---

4 Helmut Thielicke, *The Trouble with the Church: A Call for Renewal*, trans. John W. Doberstein (London: Hodder & Stoughton, 1966), 1.

5 Thielicke, *The Trouble with the Church*, 5.

6 Thielicke, *The Trouble with the Church*, 6.

when we are taught by someone we trust, when we see what is taught being put into practice before our eyes.

Writing in perhaps his earliest letter, Paul recalls, "Our gospel came to you not only in word, but also in power and in the Holy Spirit and with full conviction. You know what kind of men we proved to be among you for your sake" (1 Thess. 1:5). Paul speaks of the content of the preaching, the word of the gospel of God. Then he mentions the passion and dynamic of the presentation through the enabling Spirit. Finally, he emphasizes the character of the messengers and the evidence of the trustworthiness of their message, embodied in the consistency of their everyday lives. Whatever the contemporary challenges, in every generation and any location, only God's self-revelation in Scripture and the life-giving power of his Spirit can generate repentance and faith to bring about new birth and a transformed life. There is no alternative plan.

5

How Does the Preacher Prepare?

I HAVE OFTEN BEEN ASKED how long it should take to prepare a biblical sermon, to which I usually reply, "Well, it depends on how much time you have." The time required will vary according to the circumstances, the experience of the preacher, the length of the sermon, the complexity in the text, and so on. There are many variables. Most preachers wish they had more time to give to their preparation. On the other hand, it is possible to spend too much time and end up with so many notes and such complicated material that the end product becomes impenetrable. Like the old woman in the nursery rhyme who lived in a shoe and had so many children she didn't know what to do, preachers may have many "children" from sermon preparation that will have to be denied access to the final talk.

My concern in this chapter is to present a method of preaching preparation that does not pose impossible demands on one's time, whether in full-time or part-time ministry. In general, I have found that eight to ten hours is a workable length of time, though a little more is probably needed when one is beginning to preach. Make it realistic, and try to establish a pattern that can gradually become second nature.

Whatever amount of time you settle on, you will need disciplined control of your calendar. Preparation time must be blocked out in your schedule. It never just appears! And that means giving yourself exclusively to the task for that period of time—no emails, phone calls, social media, or other distractions. For every booking in your schedule to preach, you need a corresponding time of preparation, as non-negotiable as any other appointments. Of course, in full-time ministry, sometimes unexpected emergencies will require your attention. But preaching preparation time is the routine around which a normal work week revolves. When I was a local church pastor, my aim was to spend two and a half hours on each of four mornings in my week. In this way you can develop a workable and sustainable rhythm that can give shape to your schedule.

What follows is a suggested method for preaching preparation that I have followed for many years and found to be helpful. Please know that this is just one approach. It should not be considered the only way or some sort of straightjacket. The intention is to enable, not to restrict, so that you can adapt it to suit your own situation or develop an entirely different method. Nevertheless, I do recommend that you develop a sustainable pattern to your preparation. My approach includes four stages, spread over four separate sessions. One key factor is to learn your own maximum concentration span, per session of preparation, and then to adapt your approach to it.

Stage 1: Exegesis

The aim of this first stage is to immerse oneself in the text with as direct an encounter as possible in order to understand its meaning. The Greek verb *exēgeomai*—which means to relate, explain, or make known—is used in John 1:18: "No one has ever seen God; the only God, who is at the Father's side, he has *made him known*." The exegesis process makes known the meaning of the text to us, an essential step before we can declare that meaning to others.

There is a danger, at this earliest stage, that we may not give sufficient time and attention to the text itself. We live at a favored time in history when the number of study aids to understanding the Scripture proliferate. It is tempting to rush to the commentaries, allowing them to be the focus of our study, with the result that we preach the commentaries rather than the Bible. Similarly, although listening to others preach the text can provide the stimulus for fresh ideas and new angles, I advise not to do this first. The danger is that we adopt someone else's material into our sermon and we become content with only a second-hand encounter with the text.

Our task is not to preach other men's thoughts, however much we may admire them, but to preach God's living word. We need to receive as much as we can from the Lord through the word before we consult any human authority or mentor. Commentaries, online sermons, and other aids must play a subsidiary role and never become a substitute for listening to God speak in his word and immersing ourselves in its truth. Reliance on these aids is never a shortcut to anything but a dead end. How then should we proceed?

Read, Read, and Read Again

Start with prayer that God will give you open eyes and a soft heart as you seek to identify the original, intended meaning of this text. Then take time to read, read, and read again in your own language, using more than one translation where possible. If you know the original biblical languages, now is the time to use them. Regardless, the aim is the same—to hear the voice of the living God. As I read, I sometimes fold a blank sheet of paper into two columns and record my reactions to what I am reading under the two headings "Surprises" and "Difficulties." This helps to shape my agenda for the first stage.

Locate the Text in Its Setting

No passage that we preach just dropped out of heaven, as it were, unconnected to anything else. We should learn as much as possible about the writer, his circumstances, and the situation of those he is addressing. What kind of literature are we dealing with and what genre does it represent? Especially significant are the contextual issues—that is, where and how this passage fits within the context of its biblical book and within the context of the whole Bible. This will be addressed in greater detail in chapters 11 and 12.

Divide Up the Text and Note the Connections

This step involves subdividing the unit into its constituent parts. These may be scenes in a narrative, sentences in a theological argument, or speeches in a dialogue. But it is important also to identify the connections between these divided parts—connections that move the contents of the unit forward to achieve its purpose. This will enable you to discover how one part of the text follows from another part and how the writer makes and uses these links. This often helps to resolve the issues recorded in the "Difficulties" column encountered during our earlier readings.

Explore the Meaning of Particular Key Words or Phrases

A lexicon or Bible dictionary can help as you seek to understand the meanings of particular words and phrases in the text. Since biblical words are best defined by their usage, the most helpful route may be to discover how such vocabulary are used elsewhere, first in the book you are studying and then in Scripture as a whole. Again, it is good to do as much of this work as you can on your own, but now is the time to consult the commentaries to check your understanding and to help you when you are stuck.

Summarize the Theme of the Text in a Sentence

After we have determined the original meaning, we write a summary theme sentence as a tool to help express in our own contemporary language the core content of the text. This is not a paragraph but neither should it be a mere phrase. The summary sentence identifies the essentials: what *must* be preached from this text to be faithful to its meaning. Thus, it will guide us regarding what should be included in the sermon and what should be left out. If we spend thoughtful time and energy on the theme sentence, the sermon will not suffer from the common disease of "muddle in the middle"—that is, a lack of clarity and focus.

Having completed this exegesis stage, pray over what you have accomplished and then leave it, ideally for a day or so, to allow the content of your study to percolate in your mind and heart—even though you may be unaware that this is happening. You may want to refine the summary sentence further at the next stage.

Stage 2: Exposition

In this stage of preparation, we move from the meaning of the text— addressing the more factual questions of *what*, *when*, *who*, and *how*— to the significance of the text. This means that we shall need to dig deeper into the text with our focus on the investigative question *why*.

Because we are products of our generation and culture, we naturally tend to read our situations, presuppositions, and questions *into* the text. This can limit the significance of the text to what we invest it with. Such a reading may accord with modern literary theory, which claims that the meaning of the text exists only in the reader's perception, but that is not the way the Bible interprets itself. The text is living because it is God's enduring word, and as such it must be allowed to challenge our attitudes and redirect our actions. The notes in the "Surprises" column from our first readings (stage 1) will demonstrate this. Let me suggest five investigative questions to help guide us through our exposition stage.

What Is the Author's Purpose for His Original Audience?

Although the message of the text will transcend its original historical context because it is the living word, if we do not rightly understand its significance for the original hearers or readers—what its message was for them then—we will certainly not understand its significance for us today. So, using the notes from our exegesis stage, we now need to explore the purpose the writer had, under God, in writing this material. To identify the purpose, ask yourself what response the author wanted to produce in his readers. Then broaden out to the immediate literary context by considering what comes before and after the text under study. Are there explanations in the surrounding context that help explain the ideas and issues addressed in the text you are studying? Look for key words, repetitions, quotations, or comments that help you to see why the writer has placed the passage you are studying at this point in his book and in these words. One of the advantages of preaching systematically through a book of the Bible or major section of a book is that the purpose of the book becomes increasingly clear so that our understanding of specific sections is informed more deeply and resonates with the overall picture.

Exploring the context, therefore, not only helps determine the meaning of the text but also, for the preacher, helps identify points of application. When the context work is well done, we will have understood why the writer said these things, to these people, in this order, at this stage of the book. Another way of looking at this is to say that we are attempting to identify the transformational purpose of the passage. Scripture is never given merely to convey information; the purpose is always that people are transformed, which is why it is always "profitable for teaching, for reproof, for correction, and for training in righteousness" (2 Tim. 3:16). The basic context work we did in the exegesis section can now be developed as we begin to identify the transformative purpose of the text, not only for the original readers but for ourselves today. This will give our applications greater depth and clarity. But this leads us to a second important question.

Where Does the Original Purpose Parallel Our Contemporary Context?

When the instructions of Scripture can be applied directly to our contemporary world, they must be. For example, a statement like "the love of money is a root of all kinds of evils" (1 Tim. 6:10) does not need twenty-first-century contextualization. The love of money is a perennial human temptation.

Because of his unchanging and eternal character, there is always a strong, unbroken line of relevance between what God revealed about himself in Scripture and what it signifies for us today. Similarly, the human heart is deceitful and wicked now, just as it was centuries ago, so what Scripture teaches about fallen humanity is directly applicable to us today. But this prompts the next question.

Where Are the Differences between Then and Now?

What about when Scripture can't be applied directly to our contemporary world because of cultural, historical, or theological differences? A danger is that we might distort the significance of the text by failing to recognize the different original context and so, perhaps, interpret it in an overly literalistic manner. Consider the following example: "Greet one another with a holy kiss" (2 Cor. 13:12). This form of greeting is not literally carried out today in many cultures. Rather, we convey warmth and affection in our own culturally appropriate ways. The principle of the exhortation remains the same, but its cultural application varies.

However, it is important to remember that the principle remains. The cultural differences are sometimes emphasized by modern commentators in order to argue that the principle is no longer valid. Many of the contemporary disagreements over biblical sexual ethics and gender issues are a case in point. Some argue that such teaching is culturally grounded—reflective of a different age and ethos—and, therefore, outmoded. Scripture, however, roots its sexual ethical imperatives not in the historical circumstances of its time but in the unchanging eternal qualities of God's character and will for humanity.

Yet it is also foundational to recognize that there are important theological differences between the outworking of the old and new covenants in biblical lifestyle and behavior patterns. With the coming of the Lord Jesus and the inauguration of the new covenant, much has changed regarding the temple priesthood, sacrifices, food laws, and so on. (We will explore this theology of fulfillment—not replacement—in more detail in chaps. 17 and 18.) It is vital to read the Old Testament through the lens of fulfillment in Christ, the one to whom the Old Testament points. Therefore, we must distinguish between primary truths and secondary applications.

For example, Paul warns the Galatians, "If you accept circumcision, Christ will be of no advantage to you," because such a person is "obligated to keep the whole [Old Testament] law" and has "fallen away from grace" (Gal. 5:2–4). Circumcision is not a specific issue today for most, but the continuing principle, grounded in God's character, is that he justifies by faith in Christ and not by works of the law. The Galatians *then* were tempted to think that they could make themselves more acceptable to God through circumcision, amounting to justification by works. Believers *now* are equally tempted to make themselves more acceptable to God by their works, whether religious duties or moral achievements. One can also fall into a life of law keeping, seeking to justify oneself by legalistic righteousness, often with additional, man-made external rules being the standard of achievement.

How Do Other Scriptures Help Us See the Significance of the Text?

Since all Scripture owes its origin to one divine author, we rightly expect it to be coherent and noncontradictory, as indeed it proves to be. A key principle of interpretation is that of progressive or (perhaps better) cumulative revelation governing the whole sixty-six books. This means that later revelation provides the interpretative key by which to unlock the earlier revelation and its continuing significance. The earlier revelation is in no way deficient. But when we are interpreting the Old Testament through the lens of Christ, we want to ask not merely where he is foreshadowed in the text but what difference it makes to the significance of the text that Jesus has come. Identifying other Scripture texts that relate to the theme of our passage and then using them to illuminate its message further, by comparison and sometimes contrast, can be an invaluable tool to deepening our understanding of its ongoing significance.

How Can the Purpose of the Text Be Summarized in a Sentence?

At the end of stage 1, we sought to summarize the text's *theme* in a sentence. At the end of stage 2, writing a summary statement of the text's *purpose* will help us to be clear about what we pray God will do in our lives and the lives of those who hear our exposition. This sentence must reflect the original purpose of the text so as to focus on its continuing relevance. When you have the purpose sentence clearly written, consider prayerfully the implications of the text for the different life situations of your hearers. We cannot address every person individually, but we can think about application across the spectrums of ages and stages in life that are represented in our audience.

Summary

At this halfway point through the preparation process it may be useful to remind ourselves of the priorities that govern expository preaching:

1. The sermon is grounded in one controlling passage. The text must be in the driver's seat. While we may refer to other Scripture passages to help illuminate or interpret our text, they are not to dominate. We must ask what *this* text in its context is uniquely saying.
2. We do not impose an interpretation from outside. Rather, we dig deep into the text to discover its own authentic message.
3. Establishing the pastoral or (better) the transformational purpose of the original passage in context will enable us to explore valid implications for our situation today. Many applications may suggest themselves, but the discipline of studying the text in its context should prevent us from imposing applications

from our contemporary context onto the original. Our task is not to invent applications but to read out from the text its transformational intention and then relate that to our world today.

Stage 3: Structure and Strategy

We can summarize the goals of the preacher's preparation in two parts. First, we need to get the passage right—understanding both its meaning and significance (stages 1–2). Then we need to get it across to our hearers. Stage 3 begins the process of moving from the notes on our desk (produced in stages 1 and 2) toward writing the script for the pulpit. This will involve working out the *structure* of the talk (its contents, progression, main headings, and so on) and then thinking about the *strategy* we shall adopt to preach the truth as engagingly and persuasively as we can. My guess is that this part of preparation is often allocated the least amount of time. This may be because it is the most creative element of our preparation and can be the most arduous. We labor at the exegesis and exposition but give less thought about how we plan to land its message effectively. Returning to our theme and purpose sentences (and all the study behind them), we now need to build the bridge over which the text can travel from *them then* to *us now*. How are we going to present the message to our hearers in a way that engages mind, heart, and will? Here are some practical recommendations for preparing the outline of our talk.

Every Sermon Is a Journey That Needs a Map

Our preparation so far will have produced many observations and ideas, all of which are clamoring to be included in the sermon. But remember that the congregation will come almost totally unprepared to the passage we have spent hours studying. So we need to provide them with a road map to outline for them where we are going and some marker points to help them keep on track during the journey. The clearer the outline, the more beneficial the preaching is likely to be. Every Bible talk needs a clear line of argument that runs through it to give shape and direction to its contents. A case needs to be built. The points need to connect. That will be a touchstone for the preacher by which to decide what to say and what to exclude. This is where the hard work on the theme sentence provides its rewards.

The Outline Takes Its Shape from the Main Points of the Text

Obviously, this means that there is no one-size-fits-all methodology in producing the outline. Biblical texts come from different genres and in a variety of styles, which will demand different preaching approaches. Often, it will be best to follow the logical order of the text and replicate this in the outline. The main points of the text give you the main points of the sermon. Sometimes it may be more effective to focus on one central idea, rather like the hub of a wheel with several spokes connected to it, which lead us to and from the main idea through the subsidiary points of the passage. There is no precommitment to a traditional three-point structure, though such a structure often works well. Regardless, identification and clear statement of the main points as the talk proceeds will always help listeners.

Try to Express the Main Points Didactically, Not Just Descriptively

If the main points can be expressed as teaching or instruction, then the hearers will benefit from understanding both the content and the application of the text together. Descriptive points or headings can be limited in their impact because they may seem too abstract and remote from the hearers. A main point expressed as a teaching statement can communicate the message more persuasively and enable the hearers to more immediately engage with the text.

Teach the Truth to the Mind, the Heart, and the Will

The truth needs to be stated for the mind to understand it, explained for the heart to receive it, and applied for the will to enact it. This is the whole person response that the word of God seeks to generate.

First, the mind must be engaged by a clear explanation of the particular truth revealed in the text so that the hearer responds, "Oh, yes, I understand it now." If that does not happen, nothing will really change. Cognitive understanding is necessary for genuine transformation. Second, the truth of the text needs to be explained to affect the heart, which in biblical terms is the control center of the personality. Our purpose sentence from stage 2 will serve us well here. As we draw out the implications of the text through its exposition, the Holy Spirit can use it to soften hard hearts. Third, this makes for persuasive preaching that motivates the will to want to put into action the transformational content and intentions of the passage. But we should not assume that this will happen automatically. It will benefit the hearers if we can give some practical advice on how the application might work out in an everyday context. State, explain, apply—through the mind, to the heart, to energize the will.

Make Sure the Sermon Includes Practical "How To" Help

Christian congregations long for the Bible to be relevant to their lives. They want its message to connect, in time and space, with their lived experience. Believers have a genuine appetite for practical help, for preaching that connects. Good preaching is intellectually stimulating, but it is not complex, abstract, or merely academic. Communicating it well involves thinking hard about the objections to God's word that will likely surface and targeting the message to get under the hearers' radar defenses. This can be done by recognizing and answering questions, emphasizing the biblical motivations, and illustrating what believing and obeying this word may look like in everyday life.

If the "state" and "explain" parts of the sermon have been effectively presented, they may not need much illustration. The text will speak for itself. But the application nearly always needs illustration. "How it works out in life" is a much-valued part of preaching, and often our hearers grasp this best through illustrations of the application from real-life situations that ring bells for them because of the parallels with their own needs and experiences. At this stage in the preparation, we need to consider what applications most need illustration, how we will do that, and where they will fit in the structure of the talk.

Stage 4: Producing Your Script

This last stage of preparation is about prayerfully thinking through what you believe the Lord wants you to say (his message) as faithfully, clearly, persuasively, and powerfully as possible. The only test for preaching notes is that they enable you to do this. Everyone needs to determine the method and practice that serves them best so as to develop a sustainable pattern. There is no inherent value in either preaching with no written notes or in preaching with a full script. Both have their advantages and perils. The noteless preacher is prone to waffle, and the full script preacher is prone to woodenness. Yet the advantage with the former may be the warmth of engagement, and the advantage with the latter the persuasiveness of clarity.

In one's early days of preaching, it is probably better to err on the side of too many scripted notes rather than too few. One can easily become so focused on the act of preaching that the content is forgotten. This leads to repetition, as the preacher strives to remember what he was planning to say. For the hearers, this can be first boring and then embarrassing. Thus, a full script is best so that your mental energy can be applied to connecting with the congregation in the moment, which is more likely to happen when the points and how you want to articulate them are on the paper in front of you. But don't let yourself slip into essay mode or you will end up reading a seminar paper. Remember a sermon is intended for hearers, not readers. The two communication patterns are very different. However, whatever sort of notes you produce, you must take time to think through what you want to say and devise the best aids to enable you to do that.

Choose vocabulary that is clear and easily understood. Go for short sentences and avoid grammatical complexity. Avoid unnecessary wordiness. Give thought to the pace at which you will speak and try to vary it through the sermon. For example, if you avoid scripting your illustrations, there will be a change of pitch and pace when you come to them. Monotonously read scripts only induce sleep, but unscripted illustrations can provide variety in the presentation and keep your hearers engaged. A word of caution though: illustrations are good servants but bad masters. They can open windows in the sermon to let in light and fresh air, to aid understanding or help in application. However, if they are merely opportunities to take a breather or amusing interludes for their own sake, they will ultimately be counterproductive, regardless of the minor relief they seem to bring. The key must always be whether an illustration helps or hinders the purpose of the sermon. We must be serious without being solemn.

Scripting the introduction and conclusion are also worthwhile exercises. Some sermons lose their hearers in the first two minutes because the introductory material is dull or seems irrelevant. The opening need not necessarily be dramatic or humorous, nor does it need to be a story or an illustration. I think it can be helpful to use the introduction either as a menu of what is on offer, inviting the hearers to participate, or as a taster of a central issue to be considered, which will be resolved at the conclusion of the talk. However, it is possible to be engaging without being relevant, so what the introduction promises the sermon must deliver. Thus, it is usually much better to write your introduction last—after you know clearly where you are going in the talk and what its major points are.

Similarly, many sermons lose their impact in the closing minutes because they never seem to land. Several approaches are made to the runway, the main ideas of the sermon are revisited or even further expanded, but there is no crisp, clear conclusion. If the plane doesn't land, the potential effect is lost. The only lasting impression on the hearers is "I thought he was never going to finish!" It is much better to script a brief, pithy conclusion to drive home the aim of the sermon and provide the hearers with a compelling motivation, not only to understand and receive what the Bible text is saying but also to put its significance into practice in their lives.

When your scripting is complete, stepping away from it before its delivery, ideally for twenty-four hours, is a good idea. If you have planned your preparation sessions in a disciplined way, this will avoid the Saturday night feelings of panic that afflict the disorganized preacher. Before delivery, run through your written notes/script two or three times aloud or in your head. While doing that, consider any last-minute changes you need to make to your verbal style and use of language, as well as to the pitch, pace, and resonance of your voice and body language. We must be ourselves, not imitating or copying others but relaxed in who we are in Christ and in what the Lord has given us in our preparation. If the preacher becomes a dull lecturer or a stand-up comic, for example, the biblical message and purpose of the text will not be compelling. An earnestness without intensity, a commitment to the importance of the message being preached, needs to be evidenced in the preacher's own bearing and demeanor. It should be clear that he believes what he is saying and that it matters profoundly to him because it matters to God.

Finally, throughout the preparation process, prayer is indispensable. Start and end every stage with prayer. Pray for the Spirit's illumination and guidance at every point. Pray the word into your own mind and heart as you understand its message and seek to put it into practice. Pray for wisdom in developing the structure and strategy so that the talk will connect with your hearers. Pray for them, that God will graciously open their minds, soften their hearts, and energize their wills. Pray that God may increase, that you may decrease, and that his greater glory may be your chief concern.

In his book, *The Preacher's Portrait*, John Stott quotes an anonymous poem found in the vestries of two English churches and passed on to him by the Rev. Basil Gough of Oxford. Its words deserve to be on every preacher's desk and engraved on every preacher's heart:

When telling thy salvation free,
Let all-absorbing thoughts of thee
My heart and soul engross:
And when all hearts are bowed and stirred
Beneath the influence of thy Word,
Hide me behind thy cross.[1]

---

1   John R. W. Stott, *The Preacher's Portrait: Five New Testament Word Studies* (London: Tyndale, 1961), 111.

6

How Does the Preacher Develop?

WHILE IT WILL TAKE SEVERAL HOURS to produce a sermon, it takes a lifetime to produce the preacher. No one can create an effective Bible preacher. No process of training can ensure the quality of the end product because preaching involves many different aspects of mind and personality. However, we can be thankful that God gives his gifts of grace to the church so that within local churches there are those whom he gifts as pastors and teachers (Eph. 4:11). Mere training cannot compensate for absence of gifting, but we all have a responsibility to "fan into flame the gift of God, which is in you" (2 Tim. 1:6)—to nourish, exercise, and develop it—so that our ministry can become increasingly effective and bring glory to God.

The parable of the minas (Luke 19:11–27) reminds us that when the Master commits his resources to his servants, he commissions them to "engage in business until I come" (Luke 19:13). The good and faithful servant uses all that the Master has given him so that he may honor his trust and extend his kingdom. In this chapter we will consider seven practical guidelines as we work at our own personal development, as faithful servants, and grow in our preaching ability.

1. Recognize That You Are Not Yet the Finished Article

The preacher with a humble and healthy attitude accepts that he has much to learn and understands that the road to fulfilling any ministry is lifelong. In this sense, preaching is simply a subsection of a life of discipleship in which growth and development are constantly needed. Paul taught the Philippians,

> Not that I have already obtained this or am already perfect, but I press on to make it my own, because Christ Jesus has made me his own. Brothers, I do not consider that I have made it my own. But one thing I do: forgetting what lies behind and straining forward to what lies ahead, I press on toward the goal for the prize of the upward call of God in Christ Jesus. Let those of us who are mature think this way, and if in anything you think otherwise, God will reveal that also to you. Only let us hold true to what we have attained. (Phil. 3:12–16)

That passage reminds us that the Christian life has been rightly described as "a long obedience in the same direction."[1] In effect, Paul is saying that the mark of genuine spiritual maturity is to know how immature we remain and how far we still have to go.

Just as it is perilously easy to enter the Christian life through the narrow gate and then to settle down and fall asleep just beyond the entrance, so also it is tempting to be content with the current level of our preaching, lack an appetite for improvement, and make no effort to develop. Sports analogies are helpful here. No one wins a gold medal without supreme dedication and consistent, disciplined effort. Athletes do it, Paul says, "to receive a perishable wreath, but we an imperishable" (1 Cor. 9:25).

The potential pitfall is that we are tempted to think of ourselves more highly than we ought when God graciously uses our preaching to accomplish his purposes. Jesus told the disciples, "When you have done all that you were commanded, say, 'We are unworthy servants; we have only done what was our duty'" (Luke 17:10). God will not give his glory to

---

1   See Eugene H. Peterson, *A Long Obedience in the Same Direction: Discipleship in an Instant Society* (Downers Grove, IL: InterVarsity Press, 1980).

any human messenger. If we are to experience any degree of fruitfulness in ministry, we have to take seriously the Bible's teaching about humility and apply it resolutely to our own lives. Consider the case of Rehoboam. When his rule "was established and he was strong, he abandoned the law of the Lord" (2 Chron. 12:1) with disastrous consequences. Consider Uzziah, who was in many ways a great king of Judah. "But when he was strong, he grew proud, to his destruction" (2 Chron. 26:16). Think of Demas who deserted Paul because he was "in love with this present world" (2 Tim. 4:10) or Diotrephes who rejected John's apostolic authority because he "likes to put himself first" (3 John 9).

C. S. Lewis reminds us that it is difficult to come by humility, because we have to begin by admitting that we don't have it: "If anyone would like to acquire humility, I can, I think, tell him the first step. The first step is to realise that one is proud. And a biggish step, too. At least, nothing whatever can be done before it."[2] Many a potentially fine ministry has been brought down by pride. So we need to heed and practice Peter's admonition: "Clothe yourselves, all of you, with humility toward one another, for 'God opposes the proud but gives grace to the humble.' Humble yourselves, therefore, under the mighty hand of God so that at the proper time he may exalt you" (1 Pet. 5:5–6).

2. Review and Be Self-Critical

This is not a call to introspection but to assess our own view of our sermon after delivery. Where did it work and connect with our audience? Where did it not? We need to ask ourselves, honestly and objectively, whether the message faithfully represented the Bible passage and whether it addressed the hearts, minds, and wills of the hearers. Were parts of the talk too theoretical or abstract so that the listeners seemed lost or found it difficult to follow? Were the difficult parts of the passage explained, or were such complexities left hanging and unresolved? If you

2 C. S. Lewis, *Mere Christianity* (New York: Macmillan, 1960), 99.

were particularly uncertain or unhappy about aspects of the sermon, go back to your notes or listen to a recording to try to determine what went wrong and why.

Think back over those first crucial opening minutes of the talk. Were they engaging? Similarly, was the conclusion clear and motivational? Think about the illustrations: Did they deepen understanding or focus application—or were they just fillers? We also need to recognize where our tone may have been too shrill or where we increased our volume because people seemed inattentive. Listening to an audio recording or, better, watching a video can be painful. Nevertheless, such a review of ourselves is helpful so that we can see ourselves as others see us, paying attention to our body language, tone, pitch, and pace. But we also need to consider and thank God for instances of apparent effectiveness in which we connected the truth to our hearers. It is important to notice the positive results so that we can build on them, as well as to focus on one or two areas for improvement that we can put into practice immediately. However, remember that this is a lifelong journey. What we need most is the desire to be faithful and increasingly dependent on God who makes us grow.

3. Request Feedback from Others

Self-criticism is important and can bear fruit, but critical feedback from others who are responsible and qualified is extremely valuable. Considered and insightful feedback is rare. Many reactions to preaching are either generally supportive ("That was a lovely sermon, pastor") or negative/confrontational ("I didn't agree with what you said"). What we need to cultivate is criticism that is informed, insightful, and honest.

One way of doing this is to select a listening group—two or three members of your own congregation—who are spiritually mature and enthusiastic for the task. They should believe in preaching and be committed to your development as a preacher. Provide them with a list of brief questions to guide the discussion. If you ask for written comments, it ensures a more honest response. Make sure this set of questions enables constructive criticism, not only about the content of the talk but also about the delivery. There is nothing to be gained by vague, general enthusiasm. From the start, ask your listening group to be honest with you and not pretend that there is no room for improvement. Ask them to speak the truth in love (Eph. 4:15). The best time to receive feedback is *not* immediately after the sermon has been given. It is much better to wait twenty-four to forty-eight hours, when the critics have had time to reflect and the preacher time to recover.

Another channel of feedback is through a regular, perhaps monthly, preachers' "club," where peer group criticism is the order of the day. Four or five preachers could agree to meet together regularly, either to hear a sermon already preached by a member of the group or to discuss a sermon in preparation. The group could also share issues recently encountered in their preaching and pray for one another. We do not need to go it alone in this work. The fellowship of like-minded colleagues can be a refreshment and constant stimulus to keep us developing.

The appendix to this book includes a sample assessment that can be used by those who will provide feedback. It contains questions with explanations that I have found enormously useful over the years to enable honest and constructive responses to preached materials.

4. Cultivate Strong Relationships with Your Congregation

Much will depend on the size of the congregation or group. In large and growing churches, it becomes difficult to know everyone. But because each local church is an outcrop of the family of God—a fellowship of deep friendship, care, and sacrificial love—those who preach must be distinguished by those key relational qualities. We are not impersonal managers delivering a program. We are family. We belong to one another.

So let's develop friendships and close links with others in the church—and not only with those who share our background, ethnicity, status, age, or lifestyle. If our preaching is going to develop in a way that will help us to love, pastor, and nurture God's flock, we need to increase our emotional intelligence and sensitivity towards the whole church family. That means learning to listen, so that our preaching meets the real needs of the people in front of us. Think about where they will be at 9:00 a.m. on Monday; what they will be facing in their jobs, families, and wider relationships during the week; what challenges they are likely to encounter and what their deepest emotional issues are. If we are going to preach the unchanging word with relevance into their situations, we need to get to know them well and cultivate strong relationships with as many as we can.

Another way to develop is to think about the varied stages and states of the spiritual journeys of our hearers. The following questions may help to do this: What is the take-home value of this message to the unbelieving newcomer in church for the first time today? What about new Christians who lack assurance and are struggling with the fight against the world, the flesh, and the devil? What encouragement is there for those who are discouraged, defeated, careless, or overwhelmed by the everyday demands of life? How does the sermon help those whose lives lack focus or discipline, those who are weary and giving up, or those who feel themselves redundant and no longer needed? Considering issues like these will develop our preaching beyond the mere cognitive transfer of information to a much deeper level of heart-to-heart communication. God is not only light (1 John 1:5) but also love (1 John 4:8), and we must seek to be channels of both.

One sure way to develop the ability to convey God's word into the life situations of our hearers is by devoting time to pastoral care and counsel at the one-to-one level. There is a limit, of course, to how much an individual pastor-teacher can devote to this so that it does not affect adversely the time he must spend on his preparation and prayer. The pastoral needs will always outweigh the capacity available to meet them. But we cannot afford to separate ourselves from our people and their needs. As we are privileged to listen to people unburdening their hearts to us, we begin to learn how to better apply biblical counsel to their situations and biblical motivations to enable change.

Pastoral care also stimulates us to think critically about the controversies of our time, both within the church and in the wider culture. Because our people are facing these issues, either in their own lives and families or as they seek to share their faith with others, we cannot afford to be vague on such matters. Examples of these controversies include the relationship of church and state, sex and gender issues, marriage and divorce, spiritual gifts, addictions, music and popular culture, social media, and many more. Of course, none of us can be an expert on them all, but we need to apply a biblical mindset and worldview to these important areas and be able to articulate it when needed, not only in the context of individual care but also in our preaching.

5. Maintain Your Evangelistic Edge

It is easy for pastors, preachers, and church workers to spend almost all of their time with Christians because the needs are so many and varied. But this may cause us to communicate less effectively with those who are not yet Christians, especially as the constant flow of rapid cultural changes presents new challenges to faith and life.

The Bible preacher will greatly benefit from being involved from time to time in activities that are specifically evangelistic. This can include leading an interactive study and discussion group for non-Christians or reading through a Gospel one-to-one with an unbeliever on a weekly basis. Another good opportunity is to accept invitations to speak evangelistically in schools or in business and professional communities. These occasions are valuable in themselves, but they also sharpen our awareness of how non-Christians are thinking and what questions and objections they are raising.

Any preacher is bound to benefit from this sort of challenging exposure. It will add a cutting edge to our preaching as nothing else can. That in turn will mean that our regular hearers will have a growing confidence in inviting their friends to hear the word preached because they know that it will be engaging, accessible, and relevant. We must always prepare with the unbeliever as well as the Christian in view.

6. Reserve Time to Nurture Your Personal Relationships

The more rounded and mature I become, the better and more relevant my preaching will be. Much of what we say is inevitably a factor of our personal maturity, so this is something to develop through our network of relationships.

Let me underline again how crucial our own personal relationship with the Lord must be. We must identify and work on specific areas of weakness or ineffectiveness in our character and behavior. The quest for personal holiness, likeness to Christ, is foundational to our spiritual health. In the words of the nineteenth-century preacher, Robert Murray McCheyne, "It is not great talents God blesses so much as great likeness to Jesus. A holy minister is an awful weapon in the hand of God."[3] So we must seek to keep growing "in the grace and knowledge of our Lord and Savior Jesus Christ" (2 Pet. 3:18). Of course, this means that we nurture our relationship with him by prayer and petition with thanksgiving, as we make every aspect of our lives and ministries known to God (Phil. 4:6).

For those who are married, our priority relationships—after the Lord—will be with wife and children. We must devote time and energy to these precious God-given relationships and try to ensure that in our zeal for ministry we do not sacrifice those nearest and dearest to us. Try to be outgoing and involved with non-Christian neighbors, acquaintances, friends, and wider family. They will often judge the gospel by its messenger, so positive relationships matter not because they are evangelistic opportunities but because they are real people with real needs whom we should love and care for.

---

3   Quoted in Andrew A. Bonar, *Memoirs of McCheyne* (Chicago: Moody, 1978), 95.

Don't neglect to cultivate good relationships also with your fellow leaders, both within your own church and (as opportunity offers) in other churches in your town, area, or church association. This helps to prevent becoming narrow-minded and isolationist, only concerned with your little corner of God's kingdom.

At this point you may be thinking that if we need all of these ingredients for our development, it is an impossible task. Please realize that this is a checklist to help us grow and develop over a lifetime of ministry, but we need to get started. If we don't aim for these things, we will not hit any targets.

7. Keep Remembering the Essentials

Sometimes preaching is compared with cooking a meal. Potential ingredients have to be selected, mixed, and balanced to make an attractive and edible end product. In this view, the Bible provides the raw materials, but we have to do something with them or add something to them to create a palatable dish. But this is a misleading comparison because the ingredients are already in the shape and combination intended by God in the Scriptures. He has provided the food, and he has written the recipe. We don't have to do something with God's word. We have to let it do its work with us, in us, and then through us.

The gospel is the center of all our preaching, so we must ensure that all its essential elements are given their due weight. We begin with the human condition. Our basic human problem is not ignorance but rebellion. We live in God's world with the breath that he has given us but without acknowledging our Creator or submitting to his righteous rule. We make ourselves the center of the world and will not let God be God in our lives. The reality of human sin is an essential truth to keep proclaiming.

The divine intervention in the person of our Lord Jesus Christ coming into our world on a rescue mission is the heart of our message. In him we encounter the image of the invisible God and see how far short of his glory we have fallen. Having lived the perfect life we have failed to live, he died the death we deserve to die. His substitutionary, atoning death on the cross should be the glory of all our preaching, for by it he has carried our guilt, redeemed us from slavery to sin, turned away God's righteous wrath, rescued us from hell, and granted forgiveness and eternal life to all who repent and put their faith in him. Never move away from the cross as the foundation of all our subsequent teaching, but, instead, build on it the glorious reality of the resurrection and the expectation of Christ's return to judge the living and the dead and to consummate his eternal kingdom. There can be no compromise on these wonderful gospel realities, and we should delight to proclaim them as the life blood of our preaching ministry.

In Acts 20, while en route to Jerusalem, Paul calls for the elders of the Ephesian church to meet him at Miletus. What he says to them gives us key insights into what drove the great apostle throughout his ministry. He describes it as "testify[ing] to the gospel of the grace of God" (Acts 20:24), "proclaiming the kingdom" (20:25), and "declaring . . . the whole counsel of God" (20:27). This was how he cared for the people, which was the charge and responsibility he now was passing on to the elders. As we develop as preachers, we must maintain the same focus on the things that matter most—testifying, proclaiming, and declaring the living and enduring word of the one true God.

7

How Does the Preacher Connect?

"ALMIGHTY GOD, we bow in your presence. May your word be our rule, your Spirit our teacher, and your greater glory our supreme concern." This simple prayer, often used at the start of a sermon, encapsulates all that the preacher should long to have happen through his preparation and proclamation. The Bible text must rule or govern all that is said. The Holy Spirit is the dynamic agent by which God's revealed truth is brought to bear on minds, hearts, and wills. And as the Spirit of God takes the word of God to do the work of God, everything works together to give him glory and praise. At its heart the prayer is asking God that the preaching of his truth will connect with our hearers in a life-changing way, for the word and the Spirit to be doing their transformational work.

How are these connections to be made? Everything we have been considering thus far—the skills, hard work, and prayerful application—comes into play here. But it is only by the work of God's Spirit that this comes to its fruition in life-changing effect. Moreover, as we preach with active faith in God's living word, we can be confident that "in the Lord your labor is not in vain" (1 Cor. 15:58), because as he has promised,

> [My word] shall not return to me empty,
> but it shall accomplish that which I purpose,
>   and shall succeed in the thing for which I sent it. (Isa. 55:11)

For this to happen we need to turn our attention to three key principles, if we are truly to connect consistently with our hearers.

1. Ensure That Your Preaching Is Always Christ Centered

In his teaching to the Christians in Colossae about the nature of his apostolic ministry, Paul refers to "the stewardship from God" given to him "to make the word of God fully known" (Col. 1:25). He then unpacks the content of this open secret "hidden for ages and generations" (Col. 1:26) that he has been called to proclaim to the Gentile world. It is "Christ in you, the hope of glory" (Col. 1:27). He continues, "Him we proclaim, warning everyone and teaching everyone with all wisdom, that we may present everyone mature in Christ" (Col. 1:28).

Paul's concern throughout the letter is that his readers will come to a fuller appreciation and deeper understanding of what it means that Christ is in them so that they are not distracted or deluded by false teachers claiming to add something to the uniqueness, supremacy, centrality, and sufficiency of Christ. To advocate a "Jesus plus something" message is actually to subtract from the fullness of Jesus and to demean his person and work by making him less than the perfect revelation of the invisible God. "For in him the whole fullness of deity dwells bodily, and you have been filled in him, who is the head of all rule and authority" (Col. 2:9–10).

There are two important aspects to Christ-centered preaching that we can represent by the terms *fulfillment* and *fullness*. The word *fulfillment* gives the proper attention to the person and work of the Lord Jesus as the central reality of the entire biblical revelation. From the promise of the bruising of the serpent's head (Gen. 3:15) to the exaltation of the Lamb on the throne (Rev. 5:11–13), Christ is the unique, central, and complete fulfillment of all God's purposes. So as we preach the whole counsel of God, we will find links and pointers to the supremacy of Christ. This is most obvious perhaps in the Old Testament messianic prophecies that are expounded in the New Testament. But fulfillment is not restricted to specific prophecies. As we encounter the major characters and events in the salvation-history of Scripture, we see how they all point to a truer and better fulfillment in Christ and the gospel. Abraham, Moses, David, and all the heroes of faith point to a greater and richer fulfillment of their qualities and activity in the perfection of Christ's character and work.

Fullness reminds us that we must seek to bring God glory by elevating the sufficiency of the Lord Jesus. We must always preach a full Christ so that we never underestimate his attributes and ability. There is no part of the created order that does not belong to Christ. "For by him all things were created, in heaven and on earth, visible and invisible, whether thrones or dominions or rulers or authorities—all things were created through him and for him. And he is before all things, and in him all things hold together" (Col. 1:16–17). *This* is the Christ we must preach.

There is no area of human life and experience that does not need to be influenced by and submitted to the gospel of Christ. Every part of life in God's world is an opportunity to exercise our faith and express our worship—this includes our consistency and integrity at work, the quality of our relationships, and the stewardship of our gifts and resources. Thus, our preaching should help our hearers apply God's truth to every facet of their lives. Preaching can all too easily degenerate into a rehearsal of dos and don'ts that produces short-lived, external conformity rather than deep, life-changing transformation. We must preach Christ—"full of grace and truth" (John 1:14)—and not legalistic rule keeping. We must preach him as the eternal, sovereign, infinite, unchangeable God. Preach him as the supreme Lord of all wisdom and power, governing the world of time and space according to his good and sovereign will. Preach him as the center, not only of the Scriptures, but also of the whole history of planet Earth. And preach him as the sufficient Savior, companion, enabler, and guide for all his believing people from now to eternity. "Him we proclaim" (Col. 1:28)—the Lord of the universe and the head of his church.

Augustine famously declared, "Thou hast formed us for Thyself, and our hearts are restless til they find rest in Thee."[1] When we preach Christ, we pray for God's Spirit to activate the inner homing device in all who hear so that they might be attracted to the one by whom and for whom they were made. This is why and how our preaching has to connect Christ in all his fullness to ourselves and our hearers in all our need. Christ is surely coming! The current fallen world is not all there is. There is a bride; there will be a marriage feast; there will be a new creation. This is the ultimate perspective we must teach.

2. Ensure That Your Christ-Centered Preaching Is Always Culturally Related

In our desire to connect with our audience, we can be tempted to play down the unique aspects of our message, such as the exclusivity of Christ as Savior, the coming judgment of God, and the eternal realities of heaven and hell. The contemporary culture into which we preach will always nudge us to opt for its own values, such as novelty, excitement, or therapeutic remedies. But the Bible instructs us not to let the world distort our vision or squeeze us into its patterns. Rather we are to lovingly confront and critique the world and work for its redemption. This means that while we must communicate in ways that connect with the presuppositions of our hearers, we must nevertheless expose and challenge their views and the reasons they hold them, not condone or reinforce them.

For example, our hearers may think that there are many ways to God, that we are free to create our own sense of self and identity, or that all moral viewpoints are equally relative and acceptable. The word's unchanging, eternal truth has to be communicated into the whirlpool of contemporary life to connect with a lost world in a life-changing

---

1   Augustine, *The Confessions*, trans. J. G. Pilkington, in *The Confessions and Letters of Augustine, with a Sketch of His Life and Work*, vol. 1 of Nicene and Post-Nicene Fathers, First Series, ed. Philip Schaff (Grand Rapids, MI: Eerdmans, 1956), 63 (1.1.1), https://ccel.org.

encounter. This is why contextualization is so important. It is not about how to make Jesus relevant but, rather, to show that he is relevant. The discipline of setting a biblical text in its context so as to understand the intention of the author will enable us to draw accurate parallels to the needs, errors, and challenges of our own settings. As we determine why a particular text was written to readers there and then, we begin to see more clearly how it connects to us here and now. And what the text teaches about Christ will be the first and strongest connection from that original context to our own.

In our increasingly urbanized, fragmented, impersonal, and often threatening world, multitudes of people are longing for relationship, looking for love, and wanting to connect with others, because they are made in God's image whether or not they acknowledge it. From time to time, many people wonder whether something spiritual could provide a different, more satisfying, and lasting dimension to their lives. Yet, the relentlessness of modernity means that they are always moving to the next thing, trying the next "fix," looking for the cutting edge that will make all the difference.

If we lose sight of these realities or choose to ignore them, we will have little likelihood of connecting with people where they are. But as we preach Christ in all the Scriptures, people begin to grasp what the gospel has actually achieved—that is, the recovery, through redemption, of everything that was lost in the fall. This is especially true of our relationships—first with God himself, then with one another, and ultimately with the whole created order.

Such preaching is vital if we are to build bridges of divine truth into our secular, skeptical culture, but it is also needed within our church communities. Many Christians effectively live their lives in two different spheres; they compartmentalize the sacred and the secular. The sacred sphere comprises all that pertains to things of the soul, of eternity, of Christ and the gospel. The secular sphere pertains to everything else— the body, the mind, and daily life in the real world. This can appear to be an attractive option. The more "spiritual" you are, the more time and energy you will invest in that sphere and leave the "secular" sphere to others. Unintentionally, our preaching can proclaim a version of the Christian life that concentrates time and energy only on what is thought to be the "sacred" and that actively encourages detachment from the secular culture and gives this the label "holiness."

However, in Christ the two spheres of sacred and secular are not disconnected from one another. Yet neither are they merely connected. By Christ's incarnation, death, and resurrection, the sacred and secular are superimposed on each other. The two become one. Christ's glorious resurrection points all believers forward to the new creation and the full restoration of our redeemed humanity in the image of God. But his resurrection also brings about—here and now—renewed minds, transformed relationships, and the submission of all things (sacred and secular) increasingly under Christ's lordship. We will become increasingly in practice what we are already in God's purpose—the salt of the earth and the light of the world (Matt. 5:13–14). For our preaching to connect with our hearers, we must preach Christ as the unique, supreme, and sufficient answer to the pressing concerns, challenges, and opportunities of life today—whether at the macrolevel of the culture or the microlevel of individual lives.

We must determine, therefore, to cultivate and extend the range of our preaching, both in its biblical breadth and depth and also in its contemporary connectivity. Our biblical worldview, proclaiming Christ in all the Scriptures, enables us to apply the Bible's diagnoses and remedies to a wide variety of intellectual, social, and personal issues. At root this is because of our conviction that expository preaching *will* connect when it is driven by God's agenda and done in his way. It will relate to people's situations and their deepest needs, though they may be quite unaware of them. Nevertheless, the hearers' needs, felt or unfelt, will not be driving the sermon. Instead of starting with the agenda of the hearers' questions, the biblical preacher will begin by posing the questions that God is asking and answering through his word. These will point the way to the deep satisfaction and fulfillment that only Christ can give.

3. Ensure That Your Christ-Centered, Culturally-Related Preaching Is Always Motivated by the Gospel

The clearest example we have of preaching that connects effectively with its audience in Scripture is, of course, the New Testament Epistles. Inspired not only in their content but in their method, they provide us with wonderful examples to learn from and follow. Even a superficial survey of Paul's letters reveals the relational nature of the divinely revealed truth he proclaims. He is never simply giving information or explaining doctrine in an abstract, theoretical way. One of Paul's major purposes in his letters is to provide correction. Breathed out by God, Scripture is profitable for teaching, reproof, correction, and training in righteousness (2 Tim. 3:16). Its application requires great patience (perseverance) and careful instruction (see 2 Tim. 4:2). So how does Paul connect to the real-life challenges presented by the different churches to whom he writes? Let's consider two representative examples from 1 Corinthians and Ephesians.

1 Corinthians 5:1–13

First Corinthians 5–11 forms a prolonged section of instruction and correction, dealing with issues of morality and Christian freedom. In 1 Corinthians 5, Paul tackles an urgent issue of sexual immorality in the church. As he applies divine truth to the situation, he takes five steps that we can follow.

First, Paul identifies the problem clearly and without compromise. First Corinthians 5:1 is a bald statement of fact: "It is actually reported that there is sexual immorality among you, and of a kind that is not tolerated even among pagans, for a man has his father's wife." The identification of the problem is followed with a strong rebuke of the church, designed to undermine and correct the complacent trivialization of the sin: "And you are arrogant! Ought you not rather to mourn?" (1 Cor. 5:2). Such a scandal should have produced corporate shame and costly separation, but neither of these responses had happened.

Second, Paul states the action that must be taken. He uses his apostolic authority to prescribe what should be done (1 Cor. 5:2–5). The congregation is to act together in depriving the offender of Christian fellowship and its accompanying privileges (1 Cor. 5:2). Doing so is an act of repentance by the church, even if the offender is unrepentant. Paul uses a very forceful expression for this action: "Deliver this man to Satan" (1 Cor. 5:5).

Third, Paul provides gospel motivation for the needed action. The purpose of the church's exclusion of the man is "the destruction of the flesh, so that his spirit may be saved in the day of the Lord" (1 Cor. 5:5). The focus shifts to the eternal kingdom. What matters most is not the sinner's present comfort but his eternal salvation. The gospel governs Paul's response, as it must theirs too.

Fourth, Paul relates the issue to the revelation of the gospel. The spiritual reasons for his stance, which is ultimately rooted in the nature of the gospel, are given in 1 Corinthians 5:6–8. Using the Old Testament regulations and a parable of Jesus, he warns them through the image of leaven in bread that moral compromise will infect the whole congregation. Its purity is to be preserved because of the enormity of the sacrifice that brought the church into being. "Christ, our Passover lamb, has been sacrificed" (1 Cor. 5:7). Christ did not shed his blood in order for his people to live in moral compromise. Paul's argument is grounded in the gospel of the cross.

Fifth, Paul supports his argument with spiritual reasoning. In 1 Corinthians 5:9–13, he corrects any possible misunderstanding by clarifying that the separation the gospel demands is not from people in the world, "since then you would need to go out of the world" (1 Cor. 5:10). That would remove gospel witness from the world—a denial of the very nature of the gospel. Rather, they must separate themselves from unrepentant sinners who want to claim that they are members of Christ's body, the church (1 Cor. 5:11). God is the judge of outsiders, but they are to "purge the evil person from among you" (1 Cor. 5:13). Don't judge the world; judge yourselves.

A pattern emerges from this text (and can be traced in similar passages) by which Scripture itself demonstrates how to preach in order to connect to one's hearers in a corrective and reforming way. Pastoral preaching of this sort forms a significant part of the pastor-teacher's work, and in Paul's apostolic ministry we have a divinely given template to follow. It is important also to recognize the urgency of tone in the passage—reflected in the uncompromising language—to convince the hearers that this is not a peripheral issue but a matter that threatens the health and wellbeing of the whole church. At the same time, although the tone is urgent, it is not bullying or threatening. Paul's tone is patient and loving, full of grace as well as truth. Effective connection depends not just on what we say but on how we say it.

Ephesians 4:17–5:2

The second example comes from Ephesians. Setting the text in context helps us identify Paul's major thesis: what Christ accomplished through the gospel has not only reconciled individuals to God but has also brought together, as one body in Christ, people who would otherwise be separated from each other by irreconcilable differences and hostilities arising from race, language, and culture. The supreme example of such separation is that of Jews and Gentiles, one of the deepest and most acrimonious divisions of the first-century world. Paul's great concern, therefore, is that Christians in Ephesus will live out this gospel, especially its unity, in practical behavior and godly relationships so that Christ is glorified.

In Ephesians 4:17–19, Paul identifies the problem among the Ephesian believers: some are drifting back to their old Gentile lifestyles. He exhorts them, "You must no longer walk as the Gentiles do" (Eph. 4:17).

He then presents a kind contrast and the motivation for change: "That is not the way you learned Christ!" (Eph. 4:20). The gospel implications are expressed in a radical change of life, which conversion both demands and brings about: "Put off your old self" (Eph. 4:22), "put on the new self" (4:24), and "be renewed in the spirit of your minds" (4:23). These exhortations are grounded in the first half of the letter and Paul's exposition of the transforming power of the gospel. He then exhorts his readers to apply this teaching to their practical behavior toward one another. Their new life in Christ demands a new lifestyle.

Do you see how the pattern emerges? The problem is clearly stated, followed by the imperative to act. Motivation is supplied through the transforming power of the gospel. Then its implications for lifestyle (what it means to be renewed in mind) are worked through in a series of examples in Ephesians 4:25–5:2. In each practical example, the pattern of 4:22–24 is applied. Let's consider each in turn.

"Therefore, having put away falsehood, let each one of you speak the truth with his neighbor, for we are members one of another" (Eph. 4:25). There is a "putting off" of the old way, but such refraining from sin will only be sustained when it is replaced by positive Christian behavior. This exemplifies the "new self," the power of Christ at work, "created after the likeness of God in true righteousness and holiness" (Eph. 4:24). The motivation to change is grounded in the gospel and its effects. In this first example, putting off falsehood is confirmed when it is replaced by speaking the truth to one another. As always, motivation is found in the gospel and the renewing change it brings to the mind, heart, and will. "We are members one of another" (Eph. 4:25). Because through the gospel we have been made as one body in Christ, we belong to one another, and we must be determined not to wound the body or cause hurt to one another by failing to tell the truth.

"Be angry and do not sin; do not let the sun go down on your anger, and give no opportunity to the devil" (Eph. 4:26–27). Paul's admonishment implies that there is such a reality as righteous anger, though probably most of our anger is not righteous. But the evidence of putting off the old is demonstrated when we no longer cherish and nurture our anger but instead deal with it quickly, not allowing it to fester. The gospel motivation is that if we hold on to anger, we give the devil a foothold to hurt our fellowship with God and one another—and potentially divide the body of Christ.

"Let the thief no longer steal, but rather let him labor, doing honest work with his own hands, so that he may have something to share with anyone in need" (Eph. 4:28). Again, Paul follows the same pattern. The thief proves that he has put off stealing when he begins to work honestly for his living. The motivation is to have something to share with those in need. The thief's old lifestyle was "What's yours is mine, and I'm taking it." But the new self says, "What's mine is yours, and I'm sharing it." Only the gospel can motivate and bring about that sort of change.

"Let no corrupting talk come out of your mouths, but only such as is good for building up, as fits the occasion, that it may give grace to those who hear. And do not grieve the Holy Spirit of God, by whom you were sealed for the day of redemption" (Eph. 4:29–30). Destructive, corrupting speech is to be put off and replaced by constructive communication that shows grace by building others up. Undisciplined speech is a major cause of friction in church life, so we need a strong gospel motivation to apply the corrective. Paul points his readers to the sealing of the Spirit, the mark of ownership that identifies them as God's own people. They are destined for the day of redemption, in all its fullness, so they are to live now in light of eternity. To do otherwise would be to bring grief to God's gracious Holy Spirit.

"Let all bitterness and wrath and anger and clamor and slander be put away from you, along with all malice. Be kind to one another, tender-hearted, forgiving one another, as God in Christ forgave you" (Eph. 4:31–32). Attacks on others that characterized the old self are to be replaced by kindness, tender-heartedness, and mutual forgiveness among God's people. The motivation for these actions could hardly be more gospel-centered and, therefore, more persuasive: "as God in Christ forgave you" (Eph. 4:32).

"Therefore be imitators of God, as beloved children. And walk in love, as Christ loved us and gave himself up for us, a fragrant offering and sacrifice to God" (Eph. 5:1–2). Once again, the details are clear and uncompromising, the needed actions are specific, and the theological motivation springs from the gospel. This is a brilliant example of Paul's corrective preaching that connects with the real-life situations facing the churches. His preaching is not entertainment oriented, not topically controlled or dependent, not a devotional exercise, nor a mere comforting spiritual uplift. It is the living truth of God applied to the changing scenes of life with transforming power.

Over three hundred years ago, the New England minister Cotton Mather wrote that "the great design and intention of the office of a Christian preacher [is] to restore the throne and dominion of God in the souls of men."[2] Only a picture so grand and an agenda so vast will enable our preaching truly to connect to our people and our world. So preach Christ in all the Scriptures. Preach him as unique, supreme, central, and sufficient. Preach the word in such a way that motivation always springs from and drives us back to the gospel of God's grace.

---

2   Cotton Mather, *Student and Preacher or Directions for a Candidate of the Ministry* (London: Hindmarsh, 1726). Quoted in John Piper, *The Supremacy of God in Preaching* (Grand Rapids, MI: Baker Books, 1990), 22.

8

How Does the Preacher Persevere?

WHATEVER ACTIVITY they are involved in, many people fail to develop to their full potential because they give up too soon. Learning a new skill often begins with a burst of enthusiastic energy due to its novelty. But then comes the long, sometimes hard, road of continuous practice in which skills must be acquired through repetition. When visible signs of progress are slow (or few and far between), motivation begins to flag, energy drains, and giving up becomes an attractive option. If that happens, we will never know what might have been achieved had we persevered.

Developing into a faithful and effective biblical preacher has never been easy. To remain consistent is difficult in light of the time commitment, hard work required, and frequent lack of response. Addressing an indifferent and often hostile cultural context and a sometimes uninterested and apathetic church in a way that engages, connects, instructs, encourages, and trains in righteousness is demanding. One can be easily tempted to question whether the effort is really worth it. Many ministers effectively give up. Their time for preparation decreases, and alternatives fill their schedule. Preaching is one of many things they do but is no longer the heartbeat of their ministry in spite of the Bible's constant witness to the contrary. An undernourished congregation can quickly become anemic and inactive.

The apostle Paul understood that this was a real and dangerous temptation for Timothy, his son in the faith and apprentice in ministry. Serving as the pastor-teacher of the church in Ephesus, Timothy faced the real possibility that his isolation and the complex problems he dealt with might tempt him to give up. Paul writes his two letters to Timothy to encourage the young man to persevere in his calling. His letters are full of wisdom and instruction for us all.

Priorities for Perseverance

First Timothy is set against the background of false teaching that was threatening the wellbeing and spiritual health of the Ephesian house churches. In practice, this heresy seems to have consisted of a "spirituality" in which God's good gifts in creation were abandoned for a rigorous religious abstinence that was actually a self-justifying expression of works religion, the antithesis of the gospel of grace. Regardless of the precise details of the challenges Timothy faced, Paul's encouragement to persevere in spite of them provides an instructive series of six priorities for perseverance that are applicable to pastors and preachers in every generation.

1. Turn Away from the Folly of False Teaching

"Have nothing to do with irreverent, silly myths" (1 Tim. 4:7). Paul probably has in view the false asceticism that was invading the church. By contrast, Timothy has been "trained in the words of the faith and of the good doctrine" that he has followed (1 Tim. 4:6). The way to combat error is to fill one's mind and heart with the true word of God. We must not imagine that we have outgrown this training but persevere in digging deeper into all that God has revealed. We never have to give up the truth that we *do* know for the sake of other people's speculative ideas, however challenging or seductive they may appear.

2. Live for God and the Values of His Eternal Kingdom

Paul continues, "Rather train yourself for godliness; for while bodily training is of some value, godliness is of value in every way" (1 Tim. 4:7–8). The false teachers, forbidding marriage and requiring abstinence from foods (1 Tim. 4:3), focused on life in the physical realm, a perspective that dominates much contemporary culture, both secular and spiritual. Paul does not dismiss the body as unimportant but points to the more important pursuit of godliness, which is "of value in every way, as it holds promise for the present life and also for the life to come" (1 Tim. 4:8). The exhortation to "train yourself" includes the idea of persistence but with an eternal perspective. This is clear from Paul's comment that "to this end we toil and strive, because we have our hope set on the living God" (1 Tim. 4:10). The sure and certain hope of future glory energizes present discipline and perseverance. If we ourselves are living in light of the eternal kingdom, our great desire will be for our hearers to do so as well. If we are convinced that the true repercussions of our persistence will only be seen in eternity, we will not easily give up the enormous privilege and responsibility to "present everyone mature in Christ" (Col. 1:28).

3. Recognize Your Obligation to Be an Example to the Believers You Serve

The objective is not to elevate ourselves as model Christians, which could spell disaster. Remember the conclusion to Jesus's parable of the Pharisee and the tax collector: "Everyone who exalts himself will be humbled, but the one who humbles himself will be exalted" (Luke 18:14). We have no grounds for setting ourselves up on a pedestal or allowing others to do so. Paul's concern for Timothy is that he will "set the believers an example in speech, in conduct, in love, in faith, in purity" (1 Tim. 4:12). We will not persevere if we do not seek to exemplify in our lives the truth and values of the message we preach.

Whenever you are tempted to give up on the hard work of disciplined study and obedience, think of those who are dependent on your teaching and example.

4. Make Scripture the Heart of Your Life and Ministry

Clearly, this follows from the previous priority, so Paul underlines it in practical terms: "Devote yourself to the public reading of Scripture, to exhortation, to teaching" (1 Tim. 4:13). It is significant that Paul relates Timothy's preaching and teaching directly to the Scriptures, which are to be read in public, so that everyone knows that the source of his ministry is God's self-revelation. The word "devote" implies previous preparation in private. If the word is to be in the preacher, the preacher must be in the word, devoted to it in private as in public. It will provide the objective standard for all we seek to achieve in ministry, and it will keep us pressing on beyond our own limited and subjective targets. Scripture is where we instinctively turn to find our refreshment and energy, our vision and endurance.

What kept John Bunyan, author of *The Pilgrim's Progress*, persevering in faith and hope during the years he was locked up in an English jail for being a gospel preacher? You have only to read any of the books he wrote to see that the Bible controlled every aspect of his thinking and imagination. It was as though the Bible were flowing through his veins! That is a great ambition for a biblical preacher.

5. Practice Your Preaching Gift and Expect to Make Progress

"Do not neglect the gift you have. . . . Practice these things, immerse yourself in them, so that all may see your progress" (1 Tim. 4:14–15). The call to preach requires a commitment to lifelong practice and development, and it comes with widespread visibility and scrutiny. As we immerse ourselves in these priorities of life, others will see our progress. This incentive will help us to keep exercising our privileged responsibility with diligence, patience, and confident thankfulness. As we depend on him, the Lord will help us improve at the task. All of us have a long, long way to go, but rather than bringing discouragement, it should stimulate our perseverance.

6. Make Sure Your Life Matches What You Teach

Sometimes, to be faithful to God's word, we must teach beyond our own levels of faith or obedience. To be faithful to our hearers, we need to acknowledge our weakness and ask for their prayers. There is no shame in that sort of realism and spiritual humility. But notice Paul's words to Timothy: "Keep a close watch on yourself and on the teaching. Persist in this, for by so doing you will save both yourself and your hearers" (1 Tim. 4:16). We never take a holiday from godliness. It is not an extra but the very essence of our lives.

As we keep submitting our lives to God's word, we come to realize more and more that God does not primarily use our skills or abilities but our likeness to Christ. The more dependent we become on his daily grace, the less likely we are to burn out or give up. We can persevere because we are not relying on our own resources but on the Lord's limitless supply. We must make every effort to be vessels that the Master can use (2 Tim. 2:20–21), since there can be no substitute for the preacher's personal godliness. To that end, we must persevere.

Practical Suggestions

The priorities we have seen Paul elaborate for Timothy cannot be surpassed, because Scripture has its own unique divine authority and relevance. But using these as our foundation, there are several considerations that may help us to persevere in the everyday business of shaping our ministry by these standards. Let us consider five practical suggestions, which stem from my personal experience and observation over many years.

1. Protect Your Time for Study and Rest

If preaching preparation time is not secured in our schedules, we will have to fit it in as best we can. In practice it will be skimped and superficial, and we will become increasingly dissatisfied with the mediocre job we are doing. That kind of outcome is very demotivating. Thus, preaching preparation time must be guarded as a number one priority.

Even so, many preachers have the experience of living hand to mouth, as it were, always being pursued by the preparation yet to be done and often experiencing debilitating bouts of increasing stress on Saturday night. It is a sensible idea, therefore, to begin your initial preparation two or three months ahead of the preaching plan. For example, in the quarter between Christmas and Easter, you study the book you will be preaching in the quarter after Easter. This does not include detailed sermon preparation or writing sermon notes. Rather, it is an effort to let the word of Christ dwell in you richly. In your personal Bible study, read and reread the subject matter of the next quarter's preaching so that when you come to the detailed preparation, you will already have a head start.

Preaching preparation also needs to be augmented by other reading and study. There can be great benefit in planning a study day once a quarter or a study week once a year. The agenda for such study is not to produce sermons but to research a topic, work one's way through a new book of the Bible, or read other literature. It should be a time free from other responsibilities in which to read, think, and pray. A further extension of this principle is a sabbatical or extended leave, which is a great strategy for perseverance.

We also need to be proactive and intentional in making adequate time to rest as the corollary of our study and hard work. Rest is neither laziness nor a self-indulgent luxury. Jesus invited his disciples to go away by themselves with him to a remote place to rest awhile. "For many were coming and going, and they had no leisure even to eat" (Mark 6:31). They needed rest, and so do we. Therefore, we must schedule our rest times—a day off each week and holiday times each year. This is not just to recharge our batteries for the next round of ministry. It is a time to appreciate God's creation, to treasure and share with family and friends, and to experience whatever activity or inactivity we enjoy so that we are refreshed and energized physically, mentally, emotionally, and spiritually.

2. Plan to Read Widely

Perseverance is fostered by developing a reading program, watching selected videos, or listening to significant podcasts in order to increase our knowledge, broaden our range of thought, and deepen our perception. A preacher who is always learning will not easily bore his hearers or himself.

Begin by identifying the gaps or weaknesses in your own framework of thought. In what areas of knowledge are you vulnerable? With which genres or books of the Bible do you have little knowledge or experience? Sometimes our interest is triggered by a new publication or a wider Christian controversy. Sometimes we need to think through practical answers to pastoral questions or theological arguments to meet the challenging cultural issues of the day. Whatever the motivation, I recommend always having a book close at hand and to combine it with some reading that explores the contemporary culture in which we serve. In a rapidly changing church and world, books, blogs, websites, and videos can help us keep fresh and relevant in our preaching. But be warned and be disciplined, for they can also be great time consumers.

3. Prepare for Disappointment

This may seem a negative note to sound, but it is quite realistic. The soil often seems unfavorable, human hearts can appear impenetrable, and it can be difficult to stir the lethargic. In such circumstances preachers can easily blame themselves and begin to question their ministry role. Some degree of introspection is needed, of course, since we can be tempted to blame others for our own failures. But we should expect the work to be hard and anticipate numerous disappointments. Otherwise, why did Jesus tell us the parable of the sower (Matt. 13:1–23)? Why else does

Psalm 95:7–8 warn us, "Today, if you hear his voice, / do not harden your hearts"? Why else does the author of Hebrews exhort his readers to take care "lest there be in any of you an evil, unbelieving heart, leading you to fall away from the living God" (Heb. 3:12)?

Our hearts and those of our hearers will quite naturally harden against God's word because of our fallen, sinful nature and because "the whole world lies in the power of the evil one" (1 John 5:19). All we have to do for our hearts to harden is to hear God's word—even agree with it—but to do nothing about it. Hardness will always be the default position of the human heart.

Thank God that the Holy Spirit's ministry is to soften hard hearts. We will experience many encouragements of this sort as the word is faithfully preached, but we must be realists. Disappointments in ministry will inevitably come, and we must not despair or be disheartened when they do. Rather, we must persevere all the more, first in prayer and then in proclamation.

4. Keep in Step with the Spirit

All fruitfulness in ministry depends on the work of the Holy Spirit. The New Testament contains two prohibitions with regard to the Spirit's work: "Do not grieve the Holy Spirit" (Eph. 4:30) and "do not quench the Spirit" (1 Thess. 5:19). Both are real and present dangers, perhaps especially for preachers. In the first case, the context addresses sins of speech. The clear implication is that where speech does not build up and give grace to those who hear, the Spirit is grieved. We must beware that the motivation and tone of our preaching does not prevent the vitality and power of the Spirit from being active through it.

Quenching the Spirit is also related to speech—in this context especially to despising prophecies (1 Thess. 5:20). As God's prophetic revelation in Scripture is faithfully preached, both speaker and hearers must realize the danger that the Spirit's light or fire might be extinguished. Instead, there must be a commitment by both to listen and respond to what the Holy Spirit is saying and so to "test everything" and "hold fast what is good" (1 Thess. 5:21).

Perseverance is dependent on keeping channels open for the life-giving energy of God's Spirit to flow into the preacher's mind and heart and out to those who hear the word preached. Sometimes that process can be disrupted by sin, carelessness, or self-reliance. The way back is always through repentance. This is why we need to be at the cross, day by day, repenting of our sin and appropriating by faith the healing and restoring power of Christ's forgiveness. As forgiveness flows from his cross, so life-giving power flows from the risen, victorious Lord, made available to us through his Spirit who lives within us.

Alongside our confidence in the word of God, we must develop a growing awareness of our dependence on the enabling power of the Holy Spirit. From the first Christian sermon on the day of Pentecost through two millennia of Christian history, the gracious ministry of the Holy Spirit has used human channels to bring about conviction of sin, repentance, and faith in Christ as Savior and Lord. As Paul taught the Corinthians, "We have received not the spirit of the world, but the Spirit who is from God, that we might understand the things freely given us by God" (1 Cor. 2:12–13). Only God can do this work. Only God can soften human hearts. Only God can raise the dead to life. Only God can give power to our feeble efforts to preach, and only he can ultimately help us to persevere.

5. Immerse Yourself in God's Promises

Through the years, I have observed that the ministers who persevere and bear lasting fruit are invariably those who are unselfconscious and self-effacing. They are constantly dependent on God and his promises. Their hard work is sustained by divinely given spiritual energy, powerfully at work in and through them. So we need constantly to remind ourselves of and immerse ourselves in God's promises in Scripture—and believe them! We must pray that God will burn into our hearts the following three biblical convictions.

GOD'S WORD IS ALWAYS LIVING

God's word is the agency the Spirit uses to bring about the new birth: "You have been born again, not of perishable seed but of imperishable, through the living and abiding word of God" (1 Pet. 1:23). Scripture is the sufficient, God-given resource to bring lost men and women back to him. It is all we need to nurture and nourish us and our people as we seek to live for his glory. Trust in this great promise—that God's word has the power to bring about new birth, conversion, cleansing, renewal, and radical transformation. So persevere in preaching the word.

GOD'S WORD ALWAYS PENETRATES HUMAN HEARTS

When the Bible is preached, God's voice is heard because the Bible *is* the word of God. The author of Hebrews declares, "The word of God is living and active, sharper than any two-edged sword, piercing to the division of soul and of spirit, of joints and of marrow, and discerning the thoughts and intentions of the heart" (Heb. 4:12). It penetrates to the very core of our being. God's word is the tool he uses to wound in order to heal—to expose in order to transform. So persevere in preaching the word.

GOD'S WORD ALWAYS DOES GOD'S WORK

Isaiah 55:10–11 affirms that the word God speaks will never return to him empty but will always accomplish his purposes and succeed in the reason for which he sent it. Pore over his promises. God's word is living, active, powerful, piercing, transforming, abiding, and enduring. It will always penetrate human hearts, rescue lost sinners, and build up those who believe in godliness of character and life. God's word always does God's work, so persevere in preaching the word.

Conclusion

Our perseverance in preaching depends on strong biblical convictions about his commitment to the preaching of his word and our own total dependence on him throughout our preparation and proclamation. It is vital to allow these convictions to animate our prayers. Pray that you will live for God and the values of his eternal kingdom. Pray that God's word will be the heart of your life and ministry. Pray that God will enable you to practice what you preach and be an example to your hearers. Pray that God will preserve and refresh you, especially in times of discouragement. Pray that you will grow in your dependence on the Holy Spirit. Pray that God's living word would be active—penetrating the hardest hearts—and always accomplish his purposes. Pray that the Lord will equip you in everything you undertake for his glory.

God is the one who calls, equips, humbles, and refines us. He enables the sowing, the watering, and the growth. Amazingly, he loves to use human agents who are dependent on his equipping grace and who work hard to preach his word. Preachers are like marathon runners because the track to be covered is the whole counsel of God and the context of their application is the whole of life. We must proclaim, reason, explain, persuade, and encourage, while realizing that all our ministry in the *now* is conditioned and validated by the *not yet* of the eternal kingdom. Our lives and ministries are to be devoted to believing God's promises and obeying his commands, as we wait in faith for the return of the King, the coming of the new creation, and the crown of glory that will never fade away.

PART 2

DEVELOPING SKILLS

9

Stay on the Line

PAUL'S EXHORTATION to Timothy provides a constant challenge to the biblical preacher: "Do your best to present yourself to God as one approved, a worker who has no need to be ashamed, rightly handling the word of truth" (2 Tim. 2:15). There are several ingredients of the verse to think about. To handle "the word of truth" is a task of enormous responsibility that will be tested and approved by God himself. Everything will depend on right handling, and this clearly is the fruit of being a skilled workman "who has no need to be ashamed." The responsibility is placed squarely on the preacher's shoulders. "Do your best" implies effort, application, and hard work. The verb translated "rightly handling" (*orthotomeō*) is used only in this verse in the New Testament, but it means to cut a path or a road in a straight direction. Some commentators suggest that the background is ploughing and cutting a straight furrow. John Stott comments, " 'The word of truth' is the apostolic faith which Timothy has received from Paul and is to communicate to others. For us it is, quite simply, Scripture. To 'cut it straight' or 'make it a straight path' is to be accurate on the one hand and plain on the other in our exposition."[1]

1 John R. W. Stott, *The Message of 2 Timothy: Guard the Gospel* (Leicester, UK: InterVarsity Press, 1973), 67.

This verse implies that we must do our best to acquire and develop all the skills we can for this important privilege and responsibility. So we will concentrate now on developing those skills. Chapters 1–8 considered the foundation stones, the basic theological and practical convictions of preaching. In chapters 9–16 we move forward to the actual practice of building the sermon. Like a skilled craftsman, we need to know the tools we must use and what each adds to our competence to do the job well. The experience of using each tool effectively, in time, produces the unashamed workman. Theory must translate into practice.

The first skill, "stay on the line," was given this title by Dick Lucas in the early days of his preaching workshops in the UK, which later developed into the training ministry of the Proclamation Trust. He represented the concept by drawing a horizontal line across a sheet of paper or a whiteboard. This line represents biblical truth—what the Bible is saying in the specific passage under consideration. The preacher's task is to "stay on the line." Another way of stating this is that the preacher must "tell the truth, the whole truth, and nothing but the truth." But the ever-present danger is that the preacher will come off the line by adding to or subtracting from what the biblical text says.

Below the Line

Preaching that was "below the line" emptied many of the churches of Western Europe and the US during the twentieth century. With the continued rise of secularism, much preaching in the churches, prompted by teaching in theologically liberal seminaries, gradually eroded the Bible of its supernatural elements. The miracles of Jesus were labeled myths or dismissed as the wild imaginings of naïve, first-century illiterates. Jesus was soon designated as nothing more than a man, a great teacher perhaps, a moral example maybe, but nothing more. Creation, miracles, divine interventions, resurrection, and so forth were all irrelevant in an age of scientific realism. Although such "below the line" preaching was attempting to engage with the unbelief already present in the culture, it produced a climate of skepticism within the churches, leading to widespread unbelief. A Christ without supernatural power was not worth believing in, and even the ethic he taught would eventually be dismissed since he had no divine authority.

Preaching can also deviate below the line by downplaying biblical emphases that are out of step with the contemporary cultural mores. Thus, the burning holiness of God may be diluted in order to present a friendlier and more attractive deity. But the demise of God's holiness entails a greater tolerance for or redefinition of sin. Rebellion is transmuted into failure. Soon, God's judgment is presented as less severe or even nonexistent, and hell becomes an overstated metaphor rather than a rightly terrifying reality. The deviations multiply destructively when the preacher migrates below the line.

Above the Line

For many preachers, however, the temptation has been to go "above the line"—adding to or overstating what the Bible actually says. Such preaching tries to pull, into the here and now, all the blessings promised for God's people in eternity. The Bible speaks of a time with no suffering, deprivation, or illness. All these can be yours now, the above-the-line preacher asserts, if only you have enough faith. Perfect love, business success, personal popularity, constant victory—all are offered through this kind of preaching, and many are duped by it. Going beyond what Scripture teaches is a cruel deception that can lead to disillusionment and despair. Preaching that is above the line demands more from its hearers than the Bible does.

The Christians in Galatia to whom Paul wrote were being persuaded that the above-the-line requirements to the straight line of the gospel were needed if they wanted God to accept them. This is an age-old problem, because the default position of the religious heart is to want to add something of its own worth or merit. Preachers who go above the line, adding rules and regulations to assure us of God's acceptance, bring their hearers back under a yoke of slavery and undermine the free, unmerited grace of God in the gospel. Additions to the gospel actually subtract from the sufficiency of Christ and his work. "Jesus plus" always becomes "Jesus minus."

Faithful Stewards

The privilege and responsibility of biblical preaching is to be the channel through which God's truth is conveyed with faithfulness, accuracy, and transformational purpose. This means cultivating a humility that submits to what the Bible says. The preacher shows reverence for the Lord by rightly handling the revelation he has given. We are not responsible for its content; that belongs to God alone. We are responsible for the communication of its content, as stewards who have been entrusted with our master's resources. And "it is required of stewards that they be found faithful" (1 Cor. 4:2).

The apostles faced this sort of challenge in the earliest days of the church in Jerusalem when the Jewish authorities tried to put an end to their preaching in the name of Jesus. The question they faced was who was in charge of their speech—God or the religious authorities? "Whether it is right in the sight of God to listen to you rather than to God, you must judge, for we cannot but speak of what we have seen and heard" (Acts 4:19–20). Since we want to follow the apostolic example and be faithful stewards who speak the truth, we must do everything we can to represent that truth as accurately and compellingly as possible.

This may prove to be costly, depending on the contexts in which we minister. It may mean that your congregation will be small compared with churches where the preaching is above the line, giving the hearers what they want to hear (see 2 Tim. 4:3–5). You may be accused of being too dogmatic or old-fashioned. But this is to impose external, cultural presuppositions on the "living and abiding word of God" (1 Pet. 1:23). You may not be promoted within your denominational context if you are known to be conducting your ministry with the Bible as your foundational authority in a predominately liberal-secular ethos. There may be a struggle in your own spirit to stay faithful to God's word, since the devil will try to unsettle you, telling you that you are in a minority, that visible results are too few, or that it is not worth the time and trouble.

Practical Cautions

To help us stay on the line, we should often remind ourselves of three practical cautions.

Don't Be More Concerned with Your Interpretation Than with What the Bible Itself Is Saying

When the Bible challenges or undermines our cultural assumptions, critics will often claim, "Well, that's just your interpretation." But a detractor's comeback is no ground for rejecting the plain message of Scripture. The significance of a text is not something imposed on it by the preacher; rather, it emerges from the structure, context, and wording of the text itself. We need to be more concerned with conveying what the biblical text itself is saying rather than with how others have interpreted or misinterpreted it in commentaries. This is why we need to ask God to meet us in his word during our preparation, rather than looking to lesser, human authorities, however capable they may be. Study time is when you sort out the interpretation of the text, especially if its content or significance are disputed, but it is not necessarily helpful to include that process in the sermon. The priority of preaching time is feeding the flock with the message of the text.

Don't Be More Concerned with the Congregation's Response Than with What the Bible Itself Is Saying

During our preparation time, our instincts will sometimes tell us that our hearers will not like or accept what the Bible says because it is too countercultural, too challenging. When this happens, we are facing the issue of whether we will stay on the line. We may fear the opposition of those who reject Scripture's teaching. We may fear for our own position, popularity, or job security. But ought not the fear of God be our guiding principle? Fear of people will quickly knock us off track; instead of the Bible controlling the preaching, the congregation will. Ultimately this will mean that our preaching forfeits the divine authority that derives from the word of God alone. Remember the Bible is in the driver's seat, not the hearers.

Don't Be More Concerned with the Structure of the Sermon Than with What the Bible Itself Is Saying

Having only a superficial acquaintance with the biblical text, the preacher can be easily blown off course. An essential ingredient of preparation is marinating one's mind and heart in the content of the text. If we become too concerned too soon about how we are going to structure the sermon, we will miss the details of the passage or compromise its truth. The Bible then becomes an aid to our preaching, rather than its vital content. If the sermon construction becomes our priority, we will be diverted into wanting a perfect structure, which will make us look for power in the outline, the alliterative points, the humorous illustrations, or the passionate delivery. All these can be valuable ingredients, but when they dominate, the focus shifts to the preacher as a literary craftsman or a brilliant communicator. However, preaching the spiritual content of the message is what matters and will last, not the human packaging.

Essential Convictions

In addition to these cautions, regularly revisiting certain essential convictions will enable us to secure and develop a healthy pattern of faithful exposition.

Confidence in the Lord

We need constantly to remind ourselves, both in the study and in the pulpit, that God is with us to enable and equip us to be unashamed workers. As we submit our study and reflection to him, he will keep us true to his intended purpose, both in the exegesis and exposition of the text and also in its intended transformational application. We express our confidence by prayer throughout the process, showing our practical dependence on the Holy Spirit to be our teacher. The more dependent we are on the Lord, the more the door is open for divine illumination of the biblical text at the deepest level.

Confidence in the Scriptures

We must have confidence that the Scriptures are not only inspired and authoritative but also sufficient for "all things that pertain to life and godliness" (2 Pet. 1:3). As David teaches,

> The law ["instruction"] of the Lord is perfect,
>   reviving the soul;
> the testimony of the Lord is sure,
>   making wise the simple;
> the precepts of the Lord are right,
>   rejoicing the heart;
> the commandment of the Lord is pure,
>   enlightening the eyes. (Ps. 19:7–8)

Embracing these truths will prevent us from imagining that we know better than the Lord the message that his people need to hear. Because the Scriptures are God's own word, they are living, enduring, and powerful. They always speak to us and our hearers with their life-giving truth.

Confidence in the Preaching of the Word

We must have confidence that in preaching what the Bible says, without dilution or deviation, the purpose of the Scriptures for the church and the individual believer is being fulfilled. Preaching is central to God's purposes in bringing our lives, corporately and individually, into increasing conformity to his will. As the Holy Spirit softens hearts through the preached word, he also empowers minds and wills to trust and obey so that we live and work for his greater glory. This is why we need to stay on the line. Don't diminish or dilute the truth of the word. Don't seek to add to its message or augment it. Our task is to revere it, humble ourselves before it, and submit to its divine author by preaching Christ alone.

Let's conclude this chapter by considering Paul's declaration of his ministry focus:

> Therefore, having this ministry by the mercy of God, we do not lose heart. But we have renounced disgraceful, underhanded ways. We refuse to practice cunning or to tamper with God's word, but by the open statement of the truth we would commend ourselves to everyone's conscience in the sight of God. And even if our gospel is veiled, it is veiled to those who are perishing. In their case the god of this world has blinded the minds of the unbelievers, to keep them from seeing the light of the gospel of the glory of Christ, who is the image of God. For what we proclaim is not ourselves, but Jesus Christ as Lord, with ourselves as your servants for Jesus' sake. For God, who said, "Let light shine out of darkness," has shone in our hearts to give the light of the knowledge of the glory of God in the face of Jesus Christ.
>
> But we have this treasure in jars of clay, to show that the surpassing power belongs to God and not to us. (2 Cor. 4:1–7)

Paul mentions the danger of losing heart because gospel ministry is hard—and so are human hearts. There was the temptation, therefore, to come off the line, to change the message by tampering with the text. Another temptation was to use deceitful means in communicating—for example, to go below the line by not telling the whole truth so as to trick people into a response (2 Cor. 4:2). For Paul, the way to stay on the line is to see his ministry as a gift of God's mercy (2 Cor. 4:1) and to see himself simply as a servant for Jesus's sake (4:5).

As the gospel light shines through the proclamation of Christ, any lack of response is due to the devil's work in blinding the minds of unbelievers (2 Cor. 4:4). Only God's creative power can overcome this, so Paul recognizes that his responsibility is to preach Christ, not himself (2 Cor. 4:5), because Christ is the image of God in his glory and saving power (4:4). The light shines into blinded minds by God alone to bring people to the knowledge of the Lord (2 Cor. 4:6). Preachers are called to be "jars of clay," fragile and easily broken vessels that nevertheless carry the light of Christ, God's "surpassing power" (2 Cor. 4:7). We should never seek self-glory, which will always knock us off the line, but seek instead to glorify God by proclaiming Jesus Christ as Lord (2 Cor. 4:5).

10

Listen to the Text

ALL GOOD PREACHING begins with careful listening. As we start our preparation, it is a mistake to presume that we already know what God is going to say through the text. Instead, we must listen hard by prayerfully reading the text several times, noting both the difficulties and questions it raises and the surprises it presents that make us think more deeply about its meaning and significance. If we don't discipline ourselves to listen to the text in detail, we may have an inadequate grasp of God's message and then build our own ideas on that basis. The result will be speculation and fantasy. We will tend to preach ourselves, our agenda, or our Christian subculture, rather than the actual content of the Bible passage. We may even lead our hearers astray if we say what God is not saying. Numerous people have become disillusioned and even given up their faith when they have found that the promises made by preachers (but not by God) are not fulfilled in their lives. If we do not listen carefully to the text, our hearers will only hear the voice of the preacher and not the authentic voice of God.

The biblical text will reveal the issues that God is concerned about, both contemporary and eternal. The preacher's task is not to come to the Bible primarily to answer this world's questions about

God but to discern from the Bible how to ask God's questions to the world. In this way, our thinking is changed from our own narrow, culturally conditioned perspective to God's own priorities. He knows exactly what human beings need to hear in every generation and in every place. So if we listen carefully to the Bible and expound God's revelation through whole Bible books, we will touch our hearers' hearts and teach them the whole counsel of God. The word of the preacher lasts for a few minutes, but the word of the Lord endures forever.

All careful listening requires concentration. We must give our whole mental attention to the task in hand. Find a quiet place where distractions will be minimal. Turn off your phone and internet. If you were going to meet with the Lord Jesus face-to-face, would you be distracted by your emails? Such a face-to-face, heart-to-heart meeting is precisely what happens when you sit down to study God's word. It is not a mere encounter with an ancient text but a personal meeting with the speaking God through his living word. Begin with prayer, asking God to meet you as you listen to his word so that you are not just engaging in academic study but expecting God to speak to you. Textual analysis will, of course, have its own important role to play in our listening, but the essence of the preparation process is more like a personal conversation, full of questions and reactions. There will be things we do not immediately understand, things that surprise and jolt us out of our familiar thought patterns, things that challenge us to look at issues from a divine perspective. We have to listen hard, because out of the listening the exposition will be born.

As we immerse ourselves in the text, we often find that extraneous ideas will flood into our minds. It's useful to have a notepad nearby to act as a flyswatter so that, as these extraneous thoughts arise, you can jot them down to form a to-do list for later. This way you will avoid being diverted during your listening. Write down what you are learning as you listen, the questions and ideas that you can use as your agenda in the preparation process. Let's consider several representative passages from both the Old and New Testaments to see how this listening process may proceed.

Philippians 3:10–11

In Philippians 3:4–11, Paul explains the changes that have happened in his life since his conversion and the new priorities he now has—that is, to be found in Christ, having "the righteousness from God that depends on faith" (Phil. 3:9). He continues, "that I may know him and the power of his resurrection, and may share his sufferings, becoming like him in his death, that by any means possible I may attain the resurrection from the dead" (Phil. 3:10–11).

A hurried and inattentive reading might lead us to conclude that Paul is trusting that as he suffers for Christ in this life, he will eventually experience the resurrection in the life to come. Suffering now, resurrection hereafter. Of course, "through suffering to glory" is a great New Testament theme, but if we are listening carefully enough we may notice something unusual about the order in 3:10. It is not chronological. "The power of his resurrection" comes before "share in his sufferings." Paul refers to the resurrection before he mentions his death. That is a surprise. It seems rather odd and prompts us to ask *why*.

We must think it through. Paul needs the power of the risen Christ strengthening and preserving him if he is to endure and persevere during his present suffering. The same is true for every believer. Listening carefully to the text means that we can preach more than a generalized observation: suffering now, resurrection hereafter. Instead, we can point to and encourage our hearers with the wonderful truth of the power of the risen Christ here and now in the believer's present circumstances. The power of the risen Lord—imagine how great that must be. All his victorious energy is actually at work in us and is able to keep us faithful and persevering even in the midst of our present pain and suffering. Careful listening to the text leads to empowering application.

Isaiah 51:12–13

Situated between Isaiah's third and fourth Servant Songs (Isa. 50:4–11 and 52:13–53:12) is Isaiah 51:12–13. God's people have been pleading with him to intervene in their circumstances and bring them his salvation. God replies,

> I, I am he who comforts you;
>> who are you that you are afraid of man who dies,
>> of the son of man who is made like grass,
> and have forgotten the LORD, your Maker,
>> who stretched out the heavens
>> and laid the foundations of the earth,
> and you fear continually all the day
>> because of the wrath of the oppressor,
> when he sets himself to destroy?

In the first line, God declares himself as the comforter of his people. The rest of the two verses are one long, detailed question. God proclaims, "I am he." Then in the light of this reminder of the I AM who strengthens them, he asks, "And who are you?" This is not so much a question about identity as about attitude. They know that they are God's people, but they are acting as though they are not. One might easily adduce three failures in the behavior of God's people that the text exposes: (1) they are afraid of man; (2) they have forgotten the Lord; (3) they fear continually all the day.

Listening more carefully to the text, however, shows that the three are closely interrelated. Between the two accusations of fear stands the charge of forgetting the Lord. Following the flow of the text shows that not only does God declare that he is their comforter but also we hear of God's immense power and capacity as the "Maker," both of Israel as his covenant people and of the heavens and the earth. The question is this: if the comfort of the all-powerful Creator is available to his people, why would they fear mortal men, even those who are wrathful and oppressive? The answer, according to the text, is that they have forgotten who God really is—the sovereign and almighty covenant Lord who is committed to save his people. In other words, when we forget God, we fear men; and when we fear men, it is because we have forgotten God. When we listen carefully to the text, it reveals this insight and provides us with many areas of application to our contemporary fears and anxieties.

Acts 10:42–43

In Acts 10:1–33, Peter has responded to the God-given vision of the unclean animals and to the Gentile centurion's request to speak God's word to him and his household. As Peter concludes his explanation of the life, death, and resurrection of the Lord Jesus (Acts 10:34–41), he declares these words: "And [Jesus] commanded us to preach to the people and to testify that he is the one appointed by God to be judge of the living and the dead. To him all the prophets bear witness that everyone who believes in him receives forgiveness of sins through his name" (Acts 10:42–43).

By sensitively listening to the text, we can observe that there is more here than a mere declaration of Jesus as Savior now and as Judge to come. Although the reference to judgment is needed in order to appreciate the wonder and scope of God's great salvation, wouldn't the warning of judgment be much more appropriately traced to the Old Testament prophets? Instead, Peter says that the prophets testify to the forgiveness of sins through Jesus. Why does Peter explain it this way?

It is not uncommon to meet unbelievers who say that they cannot accept the Old Testament God of judgment but who are drawn to the New Testament portrait of Jesus as compassionate, gentle, and forgiving. But Peter puts it the other way round. All the Old Testament prophets bear witness to the forgiveness of sins available to everyone (Jew and Gentile) who believes in Jesus. And the New Testament witness to his coming, life, death, and resurrection is focused here on Jesus as Judge. Think of

Peter's hearers. They are Gentiles, led by the centurion, Cornelius, who is described as a devout, prayerful, and God-fearing man. As such he would have attended the synagogue and heard the Old Testament with its great promises of forgiveness and salvation for *Israel*. But he and his household are *Gentiles*. And yet Peter is now proclaiming that salvation and forgiveness have become available to *everyone*. How could a Gentile like Cornelius be sure of this new status of forgiveness before the holy God of Israel?

Listen to the text. If the promised Savior is also "the one appointed by God to be judge of the living and the dead"—that is, the whole human race throughout the whole of human history—then every believer can have total assurance in the face of the final judgment because the rescuer is also the Judge. This is exactly the element of assurance that these first Gentile converts would need, and it's also a strength to all God's new covenant people today. There is only one Judge, and he is the Judge of all people. But he is also the Savior, so by having faith in him we can be confident that "there is therefore now no condemnation for those who are in Christ Jesus" (Rom. 8:1). We look forward in hope, not fear, and in the assurance that our Savior who made sufficient atonement for all our sins is also our Judge who has paid the full penalty for all our guilt. These verses give us not only the narrative of the gospel events but also the solid grounds of gospel assurance.

Matthew 3:16–4:1

Sometimes the key to a fuller understanding of a passage can be discovered in a single verse or even a specific word. In the following example, by ignoring the chapter division we see that one verse—which could easily be passed over—proves to be formative in our understanding of the surrounding context. Jesus has come from Galilee to John the Baptist at the Jordan to request baptism from him.

And when Jesus was baptized, immediately he went up from the water, and behold, the heavens were opened to him, and he saw the

Spirit of God descending like a dove and coming to rest on him; and behold, a voice from heaven said, "This is my beloved Son, with whom I am well pleased."

Then Jesus was led up by the Spirit into the wilderness to be tempted by the devil. (Matt. 3:16–4:1)

The last verse (Matt. 4:1) is often read as merely the introduction to the famous temptation narrative. So we are tempted to glide past it, straight into a sermon about how to overcome temptation by relying on the word of God. But are we listening carefully to the whole text? Why did Matthew write the sentence beginning with "then"? Clearly, he wants his readers to see the connection between the baptism and what follows. Furthermore, the word "wilderness" in the same verse is also significant. Matthew wants us to make a link between the temptations, Jesus's baptism, and the Old Testament exodus narrative of Israel in the wilderness.

In Exodus 4:22, God commands Moses to tell Pharaoh, "Israel is my firstborn son." Eventually, after Pharaoh's repeated refusal to let Israel go, the Lord's ultimate judgment fell. Every firstborn of the Egyptians died, while the firstborn sons of Israel were delivered by sheltering under the blood of the Passover lamb. Afterward, the Israelites were led by God himself out of Egypt and into the wilderness on their way to the promised land. But the temptations they faced in the wilderness led to unbelief and rebellion again and again. As a result of their failure to trust, obey, and follow the Lord, Israel remained in the wilderness for forty years.

What connection, then, does Matthew want us to see? The voice from heaven has just declared Jesus to be God's beloved Son. Now, like Israel before, he faces temptation in the wilderness. But whereas Israel repeatedly sinned and failed the test, this Son triumphed. In the power of the Spirit and the word of God, he routs the devil, who attempts to seduce, direct, or conquer him. Jesus emerges as the perfectly obedient Son, tried and tested, the true Son to whom Israel pointed. Of course, there are important lessons to learn from Jesus's example in overcoming temptation, but careful listening reveals a deeper significance. By design, both sons were tested by God, but only Jesus emerged victorious. Matthew's purpose is to exalt the Lord Jesus as the perfect Son so that we can have confidence in his perfect life of trust and obedience and, consequently, in his ability to save us through his atoning sacrifice on the cross.

Genesis 6:5–9

> The LORD saw that the wickedness of men was great in the earth, and that every intention of the thoughts of his heart was only evil continually. And the LORD was sorry that he had made man on the earth, and it grieved him to his heart. So the LORD said, "I will blot out man whom I have created from the face of the land, man and animals and creeping things and birds of the heavens, for I am sorry that I have made them." But Noah found favor in the eyes of the LORD.
>
> These are the generations of Noah. Noah was a righteous man, blameless in his generation. Noah walked with God. (Gen. 6:5–9)

The opening verses of the section are all about the human condition. Note the repetition of "man." Evil has spread throughout the creation as a result of human sin. God's response is grief and pain, but he also decides to deal with the problem by blotting out humankind from the face of the earth. In this act of judgment, we see a reversal of creation. This makes the contrast between sinful humanity and Noah all the more remarkable. The words "but Noah" indicate a ray of hope; here is one man who "found favor" in the Lord's eyes (Gen. 6:8).

Alec Motyer observes that when we meet Noah he is a typical member of the fallen human race. Motyer writes,

> Like the rest, because he too is part of humankind, he is wicked outwardly and inwardly, a grief to God and under divine sentence. But in distinction from the rest of humankind a grace of God, as

unexplained as it is unmerited, has come to him. He has not "found" this grace by merit or effort; rather it has found him.[1]

Noah has no inherent right to or claim on God's mercy and grace. Instead, the rescue he is about to experience through the ark is entirely God's choice without reference to Noah's personal merit.

However, when we read the next verse, we find that Noah is, in fact, quite different from the rest of his generation. He is "righteous" and "blameless"; he "walked with God" (Gen. 6:9). So surely this must be why God chose to be gracious to him. He was worth rescuing. If we are not listening carefully, that is the deduction we will be tempted to make. If so, we will have overlooked the opening sentence of Genesis 6:9. Motyer goes on to explain that the introductory heading ("These are the generations of Noah") compels us to see 6:9 not as the explanation (of Noah finding favor) but as the consequences of 6:8—it is what 6:8 "brought forth." Seen in the light of this, the story of Noah preserves the exclusive reality of grace as grace, while at the same time demonstrating that when grace comes (6:8) it produces the changed and distinctive life of a new man (6:9).[2]

The formula "these are the generations of" is used throughout Genesis as a marker, dividing the text into sections. The noun "generations" is related to the verb meaning "to beget." The formula might be translated "this is what was generated" or "this is what came out of that," referring to an offspring, outcome, or product. Noah did not receive his salvation as a reward for his righteousness but as the free gift of the God of grace. Listening carefully to a text teaches us both that righteousness is the product of grace (as it is throughout Scripture) and also that its reception will always be evidenced and expressed in a life of practical godliness.

There is one caveat to add before we finish this skill. Beware the temptation to search for novelty, seeing something in the text that no

---

1   J. Alec Motyer, *Look to the Rock: An Old Testament Background to Our Understanding of Christ* (Leicester, UK: InterVarsity Press, 1996), 43.
2   For the detailed argument, see Motyer, *Look to the Rock*, 44.

one else has spotted and imagining that we are hearing from the text things that it is not actually saying. The test is to be able to justify our perceptions by careful evidential proof from the vocabulary, the structure of the passage, and/or the author's argument. We must be able to refer to the context—immediate, biblical book, and whole Bible. It is not a matter of clearing our minds and letting ideas jump out at us from the page and assuming that these must come from God. All of the other skills and disciplines we have considered still apply, but in his grace God can and does open our eyes to behold wonderful things out of his word (Ps. 119:18). Or, to use the metaphor of this chapter, we seek prayerfully and attentively to listen so that we may hear his voice with greater clarity and benefit.

11

Put the Text in Context

YOU HAVE PROBABLY HEARD the old saying that "a text without a context is a pretext for a proof text." In other words, you can make a text of the Bible (or any other literature for that matter) mean almost anything you want if you ignore the context. After all, one could argue that the Bible contains a proof text for atheism in Psalm 14:1: "There is no God." However, when the statement is read in its context, we realize that this is what "the fool says in his heart."

No Scripture text drops down to us out of heaven, as if it had no context. The meaning of a text is determined not only by the words it contains but also by the purpose it serves in its context—the paragraph, the chapter, the book, and ultimately the whole of Scripture. Much proof-text preaching extracts a few words from a verse and pours into them the significance and application the preacher decides they should have. But the author's—and therefore God's—intended meaning can only be properly determined by attention to context.

We need to be aware of the dangers of preaching a single verse without its context. The preacher's own agenda or dogmatic framework can all too easily operate in the driver's seat. Preaching then becomes *using* the Bible rather than being under its authority. It isolates texts rather than integrating them. Since such preaching fails to consider the wider context and compare Scripture with Scripture, the preacher will tend toward imbalance and overemphasis of his favorite themes. Biblical words have biblical meanings, in the sense that we need to examine the meaning of a word as it is used in its immediate and book contexts. Of course, it is good to check our understanding by reference to a reliable lexicon, which will give the range of meanings in various contexts, but it is rewarding to do the initial investigating for ourselves. Proof texting ultimately discourages the congregation from studying the Bible as God has given it, section by section and book by book. Rather, it atomizes God's truth and tends to reduce the Bible to an anthology of impressive quotations, instead of presenting it as a systematic exposition of God's self-revelation and a coherent guide to the whole of life.

Understanding Context

Each text we study is set in three contexts that shape, clarify, and expound its meaning and significance:

1. *The immediate context* refers to the position of the text with regard to what precedes and follows it.
2. *The book context* refers to the relationship of the text to the book in which it appears. As we bring together observations from across the whole book, we gradually become aware of its significance and major purposes—the author's big picture. Relating this whole book context to an individual passage then helps us to understand how a particular text both illustrates and contributes to the author's overall purpose.
3. *The whole Bible context* is the theological relationship of the text to the grand salvation-history narrative of the whole Bible. Examining this context helps us consider how the text points to Christ as the center of and key to the complete divine revelation.

Context study requires us to look beneath *what* the text is saying to explore *why* the text is saying it. The author's intent is never simply to give the reader information but to move beyond that to the text's personal, pastoral, and transformational purposes (see 2 Tim. 3:16). Context is a major tool for helping us understand and teach the intended purpose of the text, which in turn will provide us with its intended application. Both meaning *and* application should always be drawn from the text in its context.

Let's look at an example text and consider it from the perspective of each context: immediate, book, and whole Bible. The story of Rahab in Joshua 2:1–24 is a fascinating narrative, full of daring exploits and intriguing details. The story can readily be preached as that of an immoral Gentile woman who nevertheless responds to the truth she has come to believe about Israel's God and whose courageous actions are an expression of her new faith. She is prepared to risk her life by harboring the two Israelite spies in order to save herself and her family. She is an example of how genuine faith expresses itself through action, about the rewards of faithfulness in the midst of danger, and so on. These are very valid practical and useful lessons we can learn from the narrative, but how can the context deepen our perception and increase our spiritual comprehension?

The immediate context. The chapter begins with Joshua commissioning the spies (Josh. 2:1) and ends with the spies returning to report that the Lord had indeed given them the land as he had promised (2:23–24). When we read Rahab's rehearsal of Israel's history (Josh. 2:9–11), we see that her story is part of the much larger narrative of God's promises and mighty acts. So part of the teaching content of the chapter is that God sovereignly chooses to change the heart of a Gentile sinner, through her awareness of what he has already done for Israel ("I know that the LORD has given you the land," Josh. 2:9), and that her conversion is a key means by which he strengthens the faith of Joshua and the Israelites.

The book context. As we consider the wider spectrum of the book, which narrates the conquest of the land of Canaan, we see that Rahab models the response that would have brought salvation to any Canaanite—humble submission to God as the sovereign Lord of all "in the heavens above and on the earth beneath" (Josh. 2:11). The story of conquest could just as easily have been told with the account of Rahab omitted. So why is it included in the book? Context shows that the conquest was not about imperialism but about removing the idols and altars from the land with their gross moral perversion. Had other Canaanites turned to the Lord rather than fighting him, they too could have been rescued; but Rahab also serves as a model for how Israel should follow the Lord, living faithfully by the conviction that he is God alone in the heavens and on the earth.

The whole Bible context. Rahab appears in Hebrews 11:31 because her saving faith was exemplified by the "friendly welcome" she gave to the spies. She is mentioned again in James 2:25 as one whose justifying faith was proved to be genuine by her works. Her story, therefore, illustrates the whole Bible's consistent emphasis of salvation through faith alone by grace alone. But there is more. Rahab is a supreme example of the grace of God in action, bringing the most unlikely and disqualified into the heart of the covenant community. Not only is her whole family delivered and integrated into the life of Israel but also in Matthew 1:5 Rahab appears in the genealogical line of the Lord Jesus. A sinner and outsider could not be more welcomed by God than that. Her faith and actions not only led to her rescue from Jericho and adoption as a faithful Israelite but also put her directly in the line of redemption history leading to Christ himself. We cannot think of Rahab without realizing that God's plan was always to bring Gentiles into his kingdom so that no one is beyond his redemptive purposes. Understanding the text within its whole Bible context thus makes the application to our own lives clear: God's supreme and extraordinary grace is still at work in the most unlikely of places and people.

This example of Rahab provides a brief illustration of the sort of context work we need to do with every passage we preach. However, keep in mind that all three contexts will not necessarily be equally important for *every* text we study. Let's consider further examples, focusing on one context in each with a close-up lens.

Immediate Context

Romans 8:28

> And we know that for those who love God all things work together for good, for those who are called according to his purpose. For those whom he foreknew he also predestined to be conformed to the image of his Son, in order that he might be the firstborn among many brothers. And those whom he predestined he also called, and those whom he called he also justified, and those whom he justified he also glorified. (Rom. 8:28–30)

I have included the verses that follow the well-known Romans 8:28 since it is often quoted and preached without consideration for its immediate context. Someone in the congregation may be thinking, "Well, 'all things' certainly aren't working together for good for me. I am facing so many overwhelming difficulties. According to the verse, either I don't love God enough or I have not actually been called according to his purpose." In my pastoral work, I have quite frequently encountered this mindset in which someone has been told to believe Romans 8:28 and get on with life! The text taken out of context can be profoundly discouraging. Such discouragement was surely not Paul's purpose in writing these words—as the context makes clear.

All things do work together for good—but not for the purpose of eradicating all our problems and difficulties. The "good" that God is working in us is much greater than we realize because it is eternal in its scope. He is determined to conform us "to the image of his Son" (Rom. 8:29), to make us more and more like the Lord Jesus. This process may well be painful and, at times, we may not feel that it is for our good. But the promise of Romans 8:29–30 is that all of life's mysteries and trials are being actively used by God to mature us in righteousness and holiness and to bring us finally to our full and complete salvation. About these verses John Piper writes, "The confidence that a sovereign God governs for your good all the pain and all the pleasure that you will ever experience is an incomparable refuge and security and hope and power in your life."[1] Piper goes on to show that the chain of statements in 8:29–30 is intended to give confident assurance and security. Nothing can break it. The goal of glory will be reached because God guarantees it. Notice that attention to the immediate context has not only helped us understand the proper meaning of the verse but also given us the transformational application of glorious assurance.

Psalm 46:10

The immediate context will often help us define more clearly the meaning of certain words or phrases within the text. Psalm 46:10 is a much-quoted verse, perhaps especially by worship leaders: "Be still, and know that I am God." Is this an invitation to a time of passive inactivity—as though we are to relax and do nothing? A careful look at the context shows that the text actually calls for a much more proactive and determined response.

The eleven verses of the psalm are divided into three parts by the "Selah" annotation in Psalm 46:3, 7, and 11. We note that 46:7 and 11 replicate each other so that 46:10 is effectively the conclusion and climax of the psalm. We observe that God is the supreme focus of the text (see Ps. 46:1, 5, 7, 8, 9), while both the physical world (46:2–3) and the international political world (46:6) appear to be in meltdown. Derek Kidner aptly comments, "The psalm . . . proclaims the ascendancy of God in one sphere after another: his power over nature (1–3), over the attackers of his city (4–7) and over the whole warring world (8–11)."[2]

---

1   John Piper, *Future Grace: The Purifying Power of the Promises of God*, rev. ed. (Colorado Springs: Multnomah, 2012), 119.

2   Derek Kidner, *Psalms 1–72: An Introduction and Commentary*, Tyndale Old Testament Commentaries (Nottingham, UK: InterVarsity Press, 1973), 174.

With that immediate context in mind and in view of the rest of Psalm 46:10, what does it mean to "be still"?

We are to submit, to stop fighting against God's sovereign rule in his world and in our lives, to recognize that God is God and we are not. But to "be still" is a call to active faith, not just to let go. It involves a positive commitment of our lives and circumstances to our exalted King, however frightening and disorienting our situation. And the significance extends even beyond our own circumstances. As Psalm 46:8 and 9 demonstrate, God will be exalted among the nations and in the physical world because he is omnipotent and sovereign. However great the threats, believers "will not fear" (Ps. 46:2) because this supreme God is our "refuge and strength" (46:1).

Book Context

Mark 8:22–25

A helpful example of the book context, in addition to the immediate context, can transform our understanding of a text. This is provided by the miraculous healing of the blind man in Mark 8:22–25.

> And some people brought to him a blind man and begged him to touch him. And he took the blind man by the hand and led him out of the village, and when he had spit on his eyes and laid his hands on him, he asked him, "Do you see anything?" And he looked up and said, "I see people, but they look like trees, walking." Then Jesus laid his hands on his eyes again; and he opened his eyes, his sight was restored, and he saw everything clearly.

Questions immediately present themselves. Why is this the only recorded miracle that Jesus performs in two stages? Why does Jesus take the man out of the village so that only the disciples see the miracle? Why is this miracle recorded only in Mark and none of the other Gospels?

Plenty of suggested answers have been offered, but only by paying attention to the wider context can we really understand.

Starting with the immediate context of Mark 8, we observe that the disciples have just witnessed Jesus's feeding of the four thousand (8:1–10). They get into the boat with Jesus, and he warns them to "beware of the leaven of the Pharisees" (Mark 8:15), which they mistakenly connect to the fact that they only have one loaf among them (8:14–16). Jesus rebukes them for their lack of spiritual perception. He asks, "Having eyes do you not see?" (Mark 8:18). They are still spiritually blind.

After the account of the miracle in Mark 8:22–25, the following context contains Jesus's question, "Who do you say that I am?" and Peter's answer, "You are the Christ" (Mark 8:29). At last the disciples' spiritual eyes seem to be open. But not fully open! At once Jesus begins to teach them what sort of Christ (Messiah) he will be—one who suffers, is rejected, is killed, and after three days rises again (Mark 8:31). Following on the heels of his perceptive confession, Peter rebukes Jesus, refusing to accept a suffering Christ (Mark 8:32). At this point, the disciples do not yet see everything clearly. Their vision is impaired, like the blind man at the first stage of his healing.

Now let's expand the context to the whole Gospel of Mark—the book context. Mark 1–8 focuses on the question, "Who is this Jesus?" It takes the disciples a long time to reach the right answer, but eventually Peter gets there on behalf of the other disciples (Mark 8:29). Their eyes are partially opened. In the rest of Mark's Gospel, the question is "What sort of Messiah is Jesus?" The crucifixion provides the inescapable answer, which the disciples will not understand clearly until much later.

Thus, the healing of the blind man in two stages is actually a microcosm of the whole book. Mark records this miracle because it is an illustration of the central theme of the Gospel. Jesus takes the man and his disciples aside because the miracle is being played out spiritually in their own lives. Not only does the context answer our questions and reveal the intended significance of the text, but it also gives us our application. We must not necessarily expect spiritual sight to come quickly or suddenly. The road to faith is often a long journey of developing understanding. When we come to see that Jesus is the Son of God, the Christ, then we begin to realize why he came and how central his incarnation, death, and resurrection are to God's redemptive purposes.

Jude 24–25

Because Jude is only one chapter, it is especially helpful as an illustration of how the entire book impacts our understanding of the part. At the conclusion of the letter, Jude writes, "Now to him who is able to keep you from stumbling and to present you blameless before the presence of his glory with great joy, to the only God, our Savior, through Jesus Christ our Lord, be glory, majesty, dominion, and authority, before all time and now and forever. Amen" (Jude 24–25).

These concluding verses express a comprehensive confidence in God and his power. If they are removed from the book, they might be preached as a comforting message: "Don't worry, everything will turn out fine!" But the book context sharpens our understanding. According to Jude 3, he "found it necessary to write appealing to you to contend for the faith that was once for all delivered to the saints." The letter's specific concern is with false teachers "who pervert the grace of our God into sensuality and deny our only Master and Lord, Jesus Christ" (Jude 4). The following verses, Jude 5–16, are full of examples of those who stumbled and fell. They did so by indulging their sinful appetites rather than submitting to God's revealed will; therefore, they fell under God's just judgment. Jude's concern is that his readers are not seduced into similar patterns of behavior. So in Jude 17–23, he applies the message of the earlier verses to their daily lives. Far from being passive and laid back, they are to build themselves up in their faith, pray in the Holy Spirit, and keep themselves in the love of God

(Jude 20–21). Moreover, they are to actively rescue those who have been deluded (Jude 22–23).

The "stumbling" (or falling) of Jude 24 cannot refer to the daily mistakes we all make in our imperfect Christian lives. God's ability to keep them does not refer to an airlift-to-perfection promise for this world. As James 3:2 reminds us, "We all stumble in many ways." The great assurance of Jude 24 is much broader in its scope—namely, that God is able to keep them (and us) from apostasy. But it is balanced by the insistent command of Jude 21: "Keep yourselves in the love of God." Thus, the message of Jude is not "Let go and let God." He *will* keep us, but the evidence that is happening is that we are keeping ourselves, which means living in the light of the eternal kingdom, not seduced by the things of this world. This truth must, therefore, be reflected in our application of the verses. We can have absolute confidence that God is able to keep us in the faith and bring us to glory. And that he will do so, if we are guarding ourselves, persevering in the true faith without compromise, loving him by obedience to his word, rescuing the doubters, and contending for the faith. That is why all the glory, majesty, dominion, and power belong to him eternally.

Whole Bible Context

The most exciting and enriching use of context often occurs when we set any particular text in the story of the whole Bible, seeing how the text relates to the metanarrative of all the Scriptures and how it fits within the sweep of salvation history. Before we proceed, however, two warnings will prove helpful when considering the whole Bible context.

1. *Don't let your systematic theology eclipse the text.* It is tempting to seize on one particular doctrinal, theological, or ethical emphasis in the text and then to launch into a tour of that emphasis in the whole Bible. The sermon then runs the risk of becoming a review of systematic theology rather than an exposition of the text in its immediate and book contexts.

2. *Don't forget that biblical revelation is cumulative.* The New Testament teaches the perfect fulfillment of the Old Testament law code in the person and work of Jesus Christ. Thus, we see a progression of revelation operating in the chronological time line of the Scriptures. This is not to imply that the earlier revelation is deficient in any way but that the later revelation completes and fulfills what the earlier was pointing to. The new helps us understand the old more fully, but we are not to reestablish the old. Rather we view its unchanging truth as divine revelation through the lens of Christ.

John 2:19–21

In Jesus's early ministry in John's Gospel, we read, "Jesus answered [the Jews], 'Destroy this temple, and in three days I will raise it up.' The Jews then said, 'It has taken forty-six years to build this temple, and will you raise it up in three days?' But he was speaking about the temple of his body" (John 2:19–21).

Jesus had just expelled the traders and money-changers from the temple, forbidding them to make his Father's house a house of trade (John 2:13–17). Jesus's statement about the temple is his response to the Jews' demand for a sign of his authority to do this. Operating only from the perspective of their present time, his opponents think he is speaking literally about the Jerusalem temple, so they dismiss the saying as ludicrous. John tells us that Jesus was referring to his body so that the statement must be taken as a prediction of his death and resurrection. But the context of the whole Bible will greatly expand our understanding.

The Jerusalem temple was a more permanent version of the original tabernacle, which God had instructed Israel to build after their exodus from Egypt: "Let them make me a sanctuary, that I may dwell in their midst" (Ex. 25:8). The tabernacle was the "tent of meeting" (as was the later temple) where God met with his people to live among them. It was also the place where his people worshiped him and offered the necessary sacrifices to make atonement for their sins. Thus, in John 2:19 Jesus claims that he is the fulfillment of all that the temple foreshadowed. He is now the final meeting place between God and man, the center of all worship, the one perfect and sufficient sacrifice for sin, and the true "Lamb of God who takes away the sin of the world" (John 1:29). His death and resurrection mean that the temple has served its purpose. Jesus is now our temple where we meet with God. Furthermore, because we are united to Christ by faith, the New Testament can speak of Christians as "the temple of the living God" (2 Cor. 6:16), both corporately (1 Cor. 3:16–17; Eph. 2:21) and individually (1 Cor. 6:19). All of this is because three days after his death Jesus rose from the dead.

Mark 6:33–44

The feeding of the five thousand features in each of the four Gospels, but the perspective in Mark's account is distinctive. This is established at the beginning of the passage: "When [Jesus] went ashore he saw a great crowd, and he had compassion on them, because they were like sheep without a shepherd. And he began to teach them many things" (Mark 6:34). The shepherd theme seems to be predominant in this account, whereas both Luke and John relate the miracle more to the miraculous provision of manna for Israel in the wilderness.

The picture of the shepherd is, of course, a significant Old Testament revelation of the character of God. Israel is the flock he shepherds. Psalm 23, which opens with the famous words, "The LORD is my shepherd" (Ps. 23:1), expounds on the implications that follow from this truth. But the scattered sheep without a shepherd in Mark 6 echo the situation described in Ezekiel 34:1–6. Because the shepherds (leaders) of Israel have been feeding themselves (Ezek. 34:2) and neglecting the flock (34:4), the sheep have scattered and become food for the wild beasts (34:5). Since the shepherds have become so corrupt and irresponsible, God promises that he himself will come to be their shepherd (Ezek. 34:11–16).

Clearly, in Mark 6, this Old Testament shepherd imagery comes to its ultimate fulfillment in Christ. The promised divine shepherd has come to teach the scattered sheep of Israel the truth of God's revelation. The feeding miracle becomes an enacted parable of the spiritual food with which Christ will nurture his sheep. This is confirmed elsewhere in the New Testament. In John 10:11 Jesus declares himself to be the "good shepherd" who "lays down his life for the sheep." The cross is the ultimate proof of this sacrificial shepherd care. In the light of his resurrection, he is the "great shepherd" who is able to equip his flock with all they need to do his will (Heb. 13:20–21). Peter affirms Jesus as the "chief Shepherd" who will reward his faithful under-shepherds (1 Pet. 5:4). That shepherding role is highlighted in Jesus's post-resurrection commission to Peter (John 21:15–17), Paul's instructions to the Ephesian elders (Acts 20:28–31), and Peter's own exhortation to elders (1 Pet. 5:2–3).

For the disciples, who distributed the bread and fish that Jesus miraculously multiplied, there was the additional lesson that their future lives would be dedicated to feeding God's people with the gospel. He challenged them, "You give them something to eat" (Mark 6:37), but they had no adequate resources. Only when the disciples put what little they had into his hands did he multiply it and give it to them to set before the people (Mark 6:41). And that is what the apostles would do after Jesus's ascension—preach the gospel and feed the flock.

The wider, whole Bible context has directed our attention to a key aspect of Mark's account that might otherwise be overlooked. Jesus meets both the spiritual and physical needs of the crowd because of his compassion (Mark 6:34). This is the fulfillment of the Old Testament motif of God's shepherd care of Israel. Jesus, the great shepherd, fulfills everything the shepherd imagery anticipated. Furthermore, he continues to feed his people through his teaching, and he energizes them by his divine power.

Setting the text in its various contexts not only enables us to interpret it but also helps us better understand its deeper purposes. And as that understanding develops, it becomes easier to make the transition to its ongoing implications with confidence and penetration. Setting the text in context is a major help toward authentic biblical application.

12

Be a Time Traveler

God is an eternal, independent being. . . . His being is
without any limits. Angels and men have their beings,
but then they are bounded and limited . . . but God is an
immense being that cannot be included within any bounds.
. . . There never was nor shall be a time wherein God could
not say of himself, "I am." . . . God ever was, ever is, and
ever shall be. Though the manifestations of himself unto us
creatures are in time, yet his essence or being never did nor
shall be bound up by time. . . . What God is, he was from
eternity, and what God is, he will be so to eternity.[1]

THOMAS BROOKS

AS THOMAS BROOKS POINTS OUT so poetically, God exists outside
of time. He is infinite and eternal. But God has created time as one of
the unchangeable factors of life on planet Earth. God therefore operates within time, and he uses it to reveal himself to humankind made
in his image.

1   Thomas Brooks, "Christ's Eternal Deity Proved," in *The Complete Works of Thomas Brooks*, ed. Rev.
     Alexander Balloch Grosart (Edinburgh: James Nechel, 1866), 5:150–57.

Every part of Scripture owes its origin to a particular moment in time. Every part of Scripture is written in a particular language with a particular vocabulary and structure, which is specific to its author and his audience at that point in history. Every part of Scripture therefore is culturally and historically conditioned, but that in no way detracts from its unchanging authority as God's infallible word for us today. What we must do is establish its meaning and significance accurately and faithfully. Thus, what it meant to the original author and his audience—to "them then"—will exercise the controlling emphasis over what it will mean to "us now." We have to travel back in time to understand and expound its meaning today. We need the skill to be time travelers.

So does that mean that we have to become experts in the cultural ethos of the first-century world to be able to read and understand the New Testament? Not at all, because the Bible is God's word for everyone, not just the academic specialist. All the necessary clues for our understanding are contained within the Bible itself. "The clarity of Scripture means that the Bible is written in such a way that its teachings are able to be understood by all who will read it seeking God's help and being willing to follow it."[2]

We can be thankful that we live at a time in history when so much scholarly work has been accomplished exploring the background to both testaments, shining further light on their cultural context. Of course, as expositors we want to be as well-informed as we can be on these matters, but we must never focus on this extrabiblical knowledge over the plain meaning of the text. Nor should we think that if we do not have access to the relevant books and commentaries we cannot preach well. Rather, we can be confident that everything we need is already in the text, if we are prepared to look carefully. As we ask in prayer, God's Spirit, who is the author of the text, will illuminate our understanding

2   Wayne Grudem, *Systematic Theology: An Introduction to Biblical Doctrine* (Leicester, UK: Inter-Varsity Press, 1994), 108.

of its meaning and application today. We have to give our minds to this task, trusting him to grant us understanding.

The Time Line

Imagine a horizontal line, drawn across a page or screen, to represent human history. It begins with the creation of humankind in the image of God and continues through the centuries of human life until eventually we reach the new heavens and earth, the new creation.

God is outside of this time line, but he created it and acts within it—in deed and word, in event and explanation. From Adam onward, God spoke to man, sometimes directly as to Abraham and Moses, sometimes through his prophets. The character of God and his saving purposes are revealed through his law and through the history of his covenant people. This is the Old Testament revelation.

The writer of the letter to the Hebrews describes the major dividing point on the time line by affirming, "[God] has spoken to us by his Son, whom he appointed the heir of all things, through whom also he created the world. He is the radiance of the glory of God and the exact imprint of his nature, and he upholds the universe by the word of his power" (Heb. 1:2–3). God's ultimate revelation is his Son, Jesus Christ. Through his life, death, and resurrection, the character and saving purposes of God are revealed fully and perfectly.

However, God continued to speak through the apostles, as Jesus promised. The character and saving purposes of God, through Christ, are revealed by their testimony. This is the New Testament revelation.

That brings us to today. God is still speaking, but what he is saying is what he has said in the Old and New Testaments. The word is now complete. Nothing will be, or could be, added to it. Jesus is the complete and perfect revelation of the unseen God; there is nothing more to know of God than what has been revealed in Christ. The cross and resurrection are the accomplishment of God's saving purposes so that there is a finished work and a completed word.

How then should these convictions shape our preaching? We must have confidence in the sufficiency of Scripture to bring men and women to new life in Christ. The word does the work. As we teach the Old Testament, we must relate its message to its fulfillment in Christ because he is the focus and center of all divine revelation. As we teach the New Testament, we must focus on the grace and glory of God in Christ and not teach a system of rules and regulations. The gospel of the cross must always be the motivation and empowerment for discipleship.

We must work hard to understand, as exactly as possible, what the text we are preaching meant to its original hearers or readers. We must be especially diligent not to import today's cultural assumptions and norms into our exegesis of the text. We will not accurately convey what it means to "us now" if we have not worked hard on what it meant to "them then." When we have understood and analyzed its cultural context, we will see the timeless truth and unchanging principles that we must teach from it with much greater clarity.

We must be careful in our preaching to add nothing to the finished work and the completed word. The Lord Jesus is the perfect revelation of God (see Col. 1:15) to which nothing can be added. Indeed, to attempt to add anything would, in fact, be to subtract. He has fully accomplished God's plan of salvation through his perfect and sufficient sacrifice on the cross. Because Jesus is "the Lamb of God, who takes away the sin of the world" (John 1:29), no other sacrifice is needed for anyone, anywhere.

So our task is to be time travelers. We have to travel back to the original setting and hear God's inspired words in that time so that we can understand their proper meaning and true significance for the original hearers. Then we can travel forward to our time, with the authentic message for us, in and through God's living and enduring word.

Working It Out in Practice

Let's consider three example texts to help us work out in practice this skill of being a time traveler.

1 Corinthians 13:1–13

This famous passage is often anthologized for its literary qualities or used for special occasions (such as weddings) when an uplifting text is required. But what happens when we time travel back to Corinth?

First Corinthians 13:1–13 is undeniably a wonderful passage, a pen-portrait of love's characteristics and, therefore, of Christ himself. But we have to immerse ourselves in the time and situation of Paul's letter if we are really to hear its authentic message. What would those first hearers have made of this passage when it was read aloud in one of the house-church gatherings in Corinth? Would they have been praising Paul for his literary genius or earmarking it to be read at the next family wedding? Not at all! Some would have been angry, some ashamed, some repentant.

Paul's letter, in which our text is strategically placed, contains intense rebuke and correction. In drifting away from the centrality of the gospel of Christ crucified, the Corinthian church was becoming divided among different leaders, and they became increasingly accommodated to the secular culture surrounding them. Their values were wrong; their relationships and conduct were disordered; they were attaching far too much importance to status, human wisdom, and power. And yet they were proud of their church, their leaders, and their great spiritual gifts. If we look at the immediate context, we see that 1 Corinthians 12–14 constitute a section of the letter in which Paul specifically deals with how spiritual gifts are to be understood and exercised in public worship.

In 1 Corinthians 13:1–3, Paul mentions various spiritual gifts that mattered so much to the Corinthians. But the common denominator in these verses is that, without love, spiritual gifts have no value. Since love is the key factor, then, Paul proceeds in 13:4–8 to list love's characteristics. What he does so brilliantly is to define love in terms of what it does—actions that the Corinthians had failed to exhibit. The deeds for which Paul has rebuked and corrected them throughout the letter are all expressions of a lack of love. It is all highly ironic.

Love is patient and kind; love does not envy or boast; it is not arrogant or rude. It does not insist on its own way; it is not irritable or resentful; it does not rejoice at wrongdoing, but rejoices with the truth. Love bears all things, believes all things, hopes all things, endures all things. Love never ends. (1 Cor. 13:4–8)

By contrast, the Corinthians were proud of their gifts, jealous of one another, and dividing into factions. They tolerated immoral sexual behavior. They went to law against one another in the secular courts. They wanted to be the center of their world, and everything had to be done their way. The wealthy among them spurned and disregarded the poor. The gifted despised the ordinary and inferior. All these grievous aberrations are the exact opposite of love, as described in 1 Corinthians 13:4–8, which constitute a devastating rebuke.

When we travel back to Corinth, hear God's inspired words in that time, and understand their meaning and significance for their original hearers, we can travel forward to our time and see how Paul's stinging rebuke has penetrating relevance for the contemporary church. First Corinthians 13 is not primarily about love between a man and a woman. It is about the self-sacrificing, other-oriented, Christ-like love that should characterize our church communities. Notice that Paul uses a series of fifteen verbs—not adjectives—to describe love. He is communicating that love is about our behavior, our conduct, our actions. When we see how the chapter exposes the wrong values and relationship inconsistencies of "them then," we are compelled to face up to the similar challenges that press in on "us now." Thus, we must ask ourselves whether we are, in practice, more like the Corinthians than we would prefer to think.

Ephesians 1:3

"Blessed be the God and Father of our Lord Jesus Christ, who has blessed us in Christ with every spiritual blessing in the heavenly places" (Eph. 1:3).

This verse from the start of Paul's letter to the Ephesians illustrates how time traveling can help us understand a phrase or a key word. What does the phrase "the heavenly places" mean, and why does Paul include it? We need to examine the whole letter context.

Our first instinct may be to think that Paul is talking about what we usually call "heaven," where Jesus is seated at the Father's side and where the redeemed will one day join him. Indeed, the next time the phrase is used, we read that God "raised [Jesus] from the dead and seated him at his right hand in the heavenly places, far beyond all rule and authority" (Eph. 1:20–21). So we might conclude that Paul opens his letter with a promise of spiritual blessings in the future, when we are with Christ in his eternal kingdom.

But if we look at the immediate context, we see that Paul lists what these blessings are. We are chosen in Christ and adopted into God's family (Eph. 1:4–5); we have redemption and forgiveness (1:7). These wonderful blessings are our present experience. Then in Ephesians 2:6 Paul affirms that God "raised us up with [Christ] and seated us with him in the heavenly places in Christ Jesus." Notice the tense of the verbs. The past tense indicates a present reality. This is not something that will only come to pass in our future. We are now, currently, at this moment, seated with Christ in the heavenly places.

Paul uses this phrase on two further occasions in the letter. In Ephesians 3:10 we are told that "through the church the manifold wisdom of God might now be made known to the rulers and authorities in the heavenly places." At Ephesians 6:12 Paul writes, "We do not wrestle against flesh and blood, but against the rulers, against the authorities, against the cosmic powers over this present darkness, against the spiritual forces of evil in the heavenly places." So the phrase refers to where we are currently seated with the risen Christ *and* to where there are rulers, authorities, and spiritual forces of evil opposed to God and us. Again, what does the phrase mean, and why does Paul use it so frequently in this letter? Let's time travel to Ephesus!

We learn the details of how the Ephesian church was planted in Acts 19. God chose to do "extraordinary miracles" through Paul (Acts 19:11), because it was a city given over to occult powers, magic arts, exorcisms, and demonic oppression—in other words, Ephesus was held captive by "spiritual forces of evil" (Eph. 6:12). In Ephesus of all places, the new Christians needed to know not only that they had been saved by God's grace but also that their rescuer was triumphant over and greater than all the hostile powers that had held them in captivity. "The heavenly places" refers to the unseen realm in which the spiritual forces of evil pursue warfare against his sovereign and redemptive purposes. But "the heavenly places" is also the place where the exalted and glorified Christ reigns supreme with his people, far above all opposition.

Paul uses the phrase from the start of his letter because he knows that his readers are living in a spiritually hostile environment, where it will often seem that the forces of evil have the upper hand. So he assures the Ephesian believers that Christ is enthroned over the powers of wickedness. He has decisively conquered evil, and therefore he can rescue them from its attacks. Christ reigns over all evil, and his people are seated with him so that all the spiritual blessings they already experience are guaranteed to be theirs continually. Nothing can separate them from the love and grace of God, which are theirs forever through the triumphant resurrection of the Lord Jesus Christ. Paul's point is that because Christ reigns over evil, his people share his victory and reign with him.

The spiritual forces of evil are equally active and threatening in our own time. Sometimes they directly oppose Christ and his people, but often they act in subtle and hidden ways. As a result of our time travel to Ephesus, we can know that Christ already rules in the heavenly places. Through his cross and resurrection, he has been victorious so that everything in the created order, seen and unseen, is under his sovereign control. We do not need fresh revelation for our time. The Scriptures are complete and sufficient. Our task is to travel back to the original setting, to unpack the meaning and significance of the text, and then to apply the same unchanging message today to a very different cultural environment.

2 Peter 1:16–21

As we explore this passage, we need to determine Peter's purpose in writing to his recipients. What about his readers' circumstances prompted him to write? We know that false teachers were perverting gospel freedom into a license for sinful self-indulgence (2 Pet. 2) and that there was widespread skepticism and even mockery about the hope of Christ's return (2 Pet. 3). Peter's concern for his readers is "that you are not carried away with the error of lawless people and lose your own stability" (2 Pet. 3:17).

Immediately before our passage, Peter remarks that he is nearing the end of his life (2 Pet. 1:14–15). As an apostolic witness, he writes so that when he has departed, his readers will continue to have confidence in the true gospel, its contents, and its life-changing dynamic. Against this background, Peter describes his gospel ministry in terms of "the power and coming of our Lord Jesus Christ" (2 Pet. 1:16). This refers not only to his first coming and the power of his majesty witnessed by Peter but also to his second coming, which the false teachers were denying would happen. Peter explains that the first coming has already been witnessed by what was seen and heard (2 Pet. 1:16–18) and that the second coming is prophesied and yet to be fulfilled (1:19–21). If Peter's readers can have confidence that the first coming was not "cleverly devised myths" (2 Pet. 1:16) but the sober truth of God's self-revelation, then they can have equal confidence in the Lord's return.

So Peter invites his readers to time travel with him back to the Mount of Transfiguration (see Matt. 17:1–8) where he, James, and John "were eyewitnesses of [Christ's] majesty" (2 Pet. 1:17). They saw Jesus's glory, and they heard God's voice identifying Jesus as his beloved Son. On the basis of what Peter saw and heard, his readers (then and now) can also believe. Just as God fulfilled his promise in sending the Christ at his first coming, so Peter's readers can have confidence that the prophetic word of the second coming will certainly be fulfilled. The origin of this prophecy was not in the mind of man but from the Holy Spirit whose inspiration through Scripture acts as a light in the darkness until the full splendor of Christ's majesty bursts on the world when he returns.

By time traveling, we can see why Peter's readers needed the assurance in these verses. They faced both the hostile attacks from outside and the destructive heresies within. The crisis in Peter's day, as the apostolic generation began to die out, was whether the church would remain true to the whole gospel of God's grace. The church needed to believe in both the first *and* second comings of the Lord, without compromise, in the face of heresy and mockery. The same is true today. Time traveling enables us to preach the unchanging truth with relevance when we understand the *why* as well as the *what* of the passage.

13

Sing to the Theme Tune

EXPOSITORY MINISTRY in the regular preaching services of a local church will usually best be served by regularly working one's way through a whole Bible book or section of a book. In my own ministry as a pastor, I discovered that it was greatly beneficial to present at least an overview of the book I was going to preach before I began the series. In practice, that meant doing some preliminary preparation several weeks before the first sermon so that I was aware of the unique contribution that the book made to the symphony of Scripture.

A carefully constructed piece of music will have a theme tune, a succession of notes forming a repeated and distinctive sequence that occurs in a variety of ways throughout the composition. Each book of the Bible also has what we might call a *theme tune*. This is not to be confused with the *theme sentence* we talked about earlier (see chap. 5). The same sort of discipline is involved in sorting out the major content from the details of illustration or application, but this is now in the context of the whole book, not a single preaching unit. The theme sentence of a sermon is the big idea that must be preached in order to be faithful to the contents of the text. When we extend that concept to the whole book, we discover the theme tune—the central idea that governs the book.

The advantages that come from determining the theme tune are considerable. It will enable us to understand the major purposes for which the book was written and so give us confidence that we are working with the author's intention, rather than imposing our own ideas on the text. This gives coherence to our expositions throughout the book. Our listeners will hear the theme tune at various stages, acting as a thread running through the different passages and binding them together. Thus, they will be hearing Scripture book by book as God gave it, not just listening to our own favorite, disconnected units. Another advantage to discovering the theme tune is that reflecting on it will often present us with a key to open a detail of a specific text, enabling us to appreciate it more richly.

As we listen carefully to the text (chap. 10), consider its various contexts (chap. 11), and time travel (chap. 12), we begin to recognize the book's theme tune, giving us confidence about the coherence and unity of the constituent parts. This is both exciting and rewarding. Although good commentaries will help provide confirmation or correction, seeking to determine the theme tune in the first instance through our own study is more satisfying than relying solely on the work of others. It enables us to have a much more personal, firsthand encounter with the book we are studying. The remainder of the chapter offers four practical hints to help discover and sing to the right tune.

1. Look at the Beginning and the End of the Book

A book's beginning and end may well summarize its message and serve to hold it together. As an Old Testament example, consider the book of Isaiah. The first chapter diagnoses the appalling state of Jerusalem in the eighth century BC. Its political and social devastation was due to its spiritual apostasy. In Isaiah 1, not only is God's imminent judgment proclaimed but also his restoration that will follow. Two extracts from Isaiah 1:21–26 illustrate this:

How the faithful city
  has become a whore,
    she who was full of justice!
Righteousness lodged in her,
  but now murderers.
. . . .
They do not bring justice to the fatherless,
  and the widow's cause does not come to them. (Isa. 1:21, 23)

But God does not stand idly by. He will bring his righteous judgment, which will have a transformative effect.

Therefore the LORD declares,
. . . .
"I will turn my hand against you
  and will smelt away your dross as with lye.
. . . .
Afterward you shall be called the city of righteousness,
  the faithful city." (Isa. 1:24, 25, 26)

The faithless city is one day to become the faithful city. But how? When we fast forward to the end of the book, we find that the restoration and renewal have happened. Jerusalem has become the city of righteousness, a magnet drawing the whole earth to worship the Lord:

"Rejoice with Jerusalem, and be glad for her."
. . . .
For thus says the LORD:
"Behold I will extend peace to her like a river,
  and the glory of the nations like an overflowing stream;
. . . .
  From new moon to new moon,
  and from Sabbath to Sabbath,

all flesh shall come to worship before me,

declares the LORD." (Isa. 66:10, 12, 23)

How has this restoration happened? As you read through Isaiah, the whole book is the answer to the question: How is the faithless city to become the faithful city? It is ultimately accomplished by the coming of the Messiah and his redeeming work; only God himself can transform his faithless people. First, he is revealed to us as Immanuel (God with us) and the King who fulfills the promises made to David (Isaiah 1–31). Next, he is seen as the suffering servant, wounded for our transgressions (Isaiah 40–55). Finally, he appears as the anointed conqueror, who is both the judge of all the earth and the rescuer of his repentant people (Isaiah 56–66). This is the theme tune of Isaiah that binds the book together: only God can transform his faithless people, and he will do so through his Messiah.

Let's also consider a New Testament example. In the prologue to John's Gospel (John 1:1–18), the dominant note is the appearance of the Word and what we need to know about his personal identity. His origin is eternal and divine (John 1:1–2). He is the agent of creation, the power of life and light (1:3–5). His mission is to give the right to become children of God (John 1:12) and to reveal the character of the unseen God (1:14). It is not until John 1:17 that the Word is given a name—Jesus Christ. Between the two major revelatory passages (John 1:1–5 and 1:14) is a section introducing the necessity of human witness in the person of John the Baptist (1:6–8). The prologue has introduced us to who Jesus is: the light shining in the darkness and the Word made flesh who dwelt among us. This is the substance of John the Baptist's witness so that those who believed in Jesus received life, as they were born again by the will of God and became his children (John 1:12–13).

Toward the end of the Gospel, John includes a purpose statement that echoes the ideas of the beginning: "Now Jesus did many other signs in the presence of his disciples, which are not written in this book;

but these are written so that you may believe that Jesus is the Christ, the Son of God, and that by believing you may have life in his name" (John 20:30–31). Note the same ingredients—evidence, faith, and life. The Gospel's theme tune has been to record the evidence (verbal and visual) by which the true identity of Jesus has been revealed. The evidence is given to generate faith, and the outcome of that faith is eternal life. All the way through the Gospel that theme tune plays. What other explanation is there for the matchless words and mighty deeds of Jesus than that he is the eternal Word, the true light, the Son of God?

Another New Testament example is Paul's magisterial letter to the Romans. In the opening verses (Rom. 1:1–6), Paul focuses on "the gospel of God," promised in the Old Testament, fulfilled in the risen Christ, to be proclaimed to all the nations so that they might be brought to the obedience of faith. All of these elements are repeated as the letter ends (Rom. 16:25–27). We shall not go wrong, therefore, if we listen for these elements of the theme tune throughout the letter. Then we shall not preach each section of the letter as disconnected, individual notes but as vital parts of a unified and coherent whole.

2. Look for Signposts within the Book

On occasion, the biblical author provides signposts as to how he has structured his material, which serve as clues about the theme tune—either for the book or for a section of the book. For example, Matthew 4:23 describes the start of Jesus's ministry: "And he went throughout all Galilee, teaching in their synagogues and proclaiming the gospel of the kingdom and healing every disease and every affliction among the people." When we reach Matthew 9:35, the wording is almost identical: "And Jesus went throughout all the cities and villages, teaching in their synagogues and proclaiming the gospel of the kingdom and healing every disease and every affliction." Matthew is a skilled craftsman who wants us to see these verses as signposts, indicating that everything between them is a coherent and self-contained unit. Both verses speak of Jesus teaching, proclaiming, and healing. And that is the content of this unit, which consists of the Sermon on the Mount (Matt. 5–7) and a long series of healing miracles (Matt. 8–9). The theme tune of this section is clear: the focus of the Galilean ministry is on what Jesus said and did. Thus, when we preach these chapters, we must sing to that tune.

Sometimes such signposts set off a single chapter. For example, consider Luke 15, which includes the three parables of the lost sheep, the lost coin, and the lost son. The chapter begins with the Pharisees grumbling about Jesus receiving and eating with sinners, and it ends with the older brother in the parable of the lost son refusing to join the feast to celebrate his brother's repentance and restoration. Table fellowship (eating together) is a mark of acceptance and relationship that Jesus offers to all who draw near to hear him (Luke 15:1–2). But the Pharisees, like the older brother, have no time for repentant sinners because they are full of self-righteous entitlement to God's blessings. Identifying the signposts helps us treat the chapter as a unified whole and discover the theme tune: God is especially concerned to rescue the lost and bring them back into a right relationship with him.

Work of this sort prevents us from reducing the impact of the parables. In a parable, the emphasis most frequently comes at the end, alerting us to its main point. The sheep, the coin, and the prodigal son are not the main focus of interest. The focus is, rather, on the shepherd, the woman, and the father who are seeking what was lost. Furthermore, the third parable also focuses on the older brother—representing the attitude of the Pharisees—who objects to the father's joyful reception and forgiveness extended to such an "outsider." But what could be further from the heart of God?

3. Look for Repetition of Thought and Vocabulary

Another practical hint to help determine the theme tune is to look for repeated ideas and words. Let's look at Paul's letter to the Colossians. In the first two chapters, we find multiple references to fullness / being filled, completeness, maturity, and so on. A survey of the letter shows that these related concepts are more numerous here than in any other of Paul's letters, so they must be significant. If we examine the occurrences of these words, we will find that most of them refer to Christ or to the Colossians.

For example, in Colossians 1:9, Paul is praying that they "may be *filled* with the knowledge of [God's] will." He wants them to "reach all the riches of *full* assurance of understanding" (Col. 2:2) and to realize that they "have been *filled* in him, who is the head of all rule and authority" (2:10). Such knowledge will mean that he is able to "present everyone *mature* in Christ" (Col. 1:28). This teaching is grounded in the matching references to the supremacy and total sufficiency of the Lord Jesus. "For in him all the *fullness* of God was pleased to dwell" (Col. 1:19); "for in him the whole *fullness* of deity dwells bodily" (2:9). You could not have greater fullness than that.

So the letter brings the two strands together. As we note these repetitive emphases, the theme tune begins to play—everything we need for spiritual fullness is already ours through faith in Christ. This is played out against the background of distortions and distractions by which the Colossians are in danger of being duped. Paul writes so that no one may delude them (Col. 2:4, 8). He warns them not to submit to religious regulations or to ascetic practices "according to human precepts and teachings" (Col. 2:22). "These are a shadow of the things to come, but the substance belongs to Christ" (Col. 2:17). In other words, they do not need a new spirituality or to seek some additional "fullness," because they are already complete in Christ. Preaching through the letter by singing the theme tune, we come to understand that the attempt to add anything to Christ actually subtracts from him.

Under the section on signposts above, we identified the theme tune in John's Gospel. It is interesting to reflect on how an awareness of that may open a deeper understanding of details within the Gospel. Take John 20, for example. The chapter is divided into four sections, each focusing on a resurrection narrative. Note the repetition. Mary came and saw (John 20:1). John ("the other disciple") reached the tomb and saw (20:4–5). Peter went in and saw (20:6). Then John went in, saw, and believed (20:8). Mary saw the two angels and Jesus (20:12, 14), so she told the disciples, "I have seen the Lord" (20:18). The disciples saw Jesus (20:20) and tell Thomas, "We have seen the Lord" (20:25). But Thomas answered, "Unless I see . . . I will never believe" (20:25). Jesus told him, "Have you believed because you have seen me? Blessed are those who have not seen and yet have believed" (20:29).

John 20 clearly repeats the relationship between seeing and believing. The disciples see and believe. Is it then unreasonable for Thomas to insist on the same privilege? At one level it is not, because he is to become an apostolic witness to the risen Lord. But in this context, Jesus rebukes his unbelief. For Thomas, "seeing is believing" because, as John tells us, the disciples "did not understand the Scripture, that he must rise from the dead" (John 20:9). But there is another way to believe. If we have been listening to John's theme tune, we know that for every succeeding generation of believers, faith will come through the apostolic testimony. Thomas is rebuked because he did not believe the testimony of the apostles. We believe because they saw. On their witness our faith is built.

4. Look for the Surprises

Whenever we come across something strange in a biblical text, it can prompt us to dig more deeply to understand what the author is communicating. Exploring such surprises can be another means of discovering the theme tune. This happened to me some years ago when I was preparing an expository series in the Gospel of Luke. In Luke 1:2, I was surprised to find the author referring to the apostolic eyewitnesses of Jesus as "ministers of the word." I would have expected "ministers of the Lord." So I set myself to explore both the use of "word" in the Gospel and the instances where Jesus speaks with power to accomplish his will. I began to hear a theme tune playing. The major events by which Luke builds his picture of the Lord Jesus and his ministry are dependent on the power of God's word. God achieves his purposes through his powerful word.

In Luke 1, the focus is on the contrast between Zechariah, the father of John the Baptist, and Mary, the mother of Jesus. Both receive visits from the angel Gabriel with a message from God concerning the roles they are to fulfill in redemption history. Zechariah does not believe and is struck dumb, but Mary responds, "Behold, I am the servant of the Lord; let it be to me according to your word" (Luke 1:38). To be the Lord's servant is to be the servant of his powerful word, by which his will is revealed and his purposes advanced. And so it goes on. In Luke 2, the shepherds receive the word from God through the angel of the Lord concerning the Messiah's birth. When they believe and obey the word, they discover the baby in the manger and return "glorifying and praising God for all they had heard and seen, as it had been told them" (Luke 2:20). In the temptation narrative (Luke 4:1–13), the devil is defeated by the power of God's word. Jesus begins his ministry in the Nazareth synagogue by revealing himself as the one who proclaims God's word—the good news of salvation (Luke 4:16–21). Peter makes a huge catch of fish because he is obedient to Jesus's word (Luke 5:5–6). Jesus heals the paralyzed man and forgives his sins by his word (Luke 5:17–26). Levi's life is transformed by submitting to Jesus's powerful word (Luke 5:27–28). The theme continues in scene after scene.

God's word is powerful to reveal and to accomplish his purposes. That is the theme tune playing through all these episodes in Luke's Gospel. So when we come to the final chapter with the post-resurrection appearances of Jesus, it is no surprise to hear the theme tune still playing. With the two on the road to Emmaus, "beginning with Moses and all the Prophets, he interpreted to them in all the Scriptures the things concerning himself" (Luke 24:27). To the disciples he said, "These are my words that I spoke to you while I was still with you, that everything written about me in the Law of Moses and the Prophets and the Psalms must be fulfilled. Then he opened their minds to understand the Scriptures" (Luke 24:44–45). As we preach through the Gospel, we shall be drawing out the implications of this theme tune. God's word did and does accomplish his purposes. God's word requires a response of wholehearted commitment and obedience. God's word will always bring glory to the Lord Jesus and will be the means by which lives are transformed and his kingdom is built.

As we study books of the Bible, we will find many amazing and beautiful theme tunes. But the approaches discussed above will greatly help our understanding and discernment about the unique purpose and application of each book. The theme tune in Genesis teaches us God's unremitting faithfulness in working out his salvation plan in the face of human sin and rebellion. In Ruth, the theme is the irresistible providence and gracious provision of God for his people. In 1 Peter the theme tune is the true grace of God in the gospel, which is the solid foundation for Christian perseverance in the face of hostility and persecution. With sixty-six books in Scripture, discovering their theme tunes is a lifetime's agenda of work for every Bible teacher. But how much stronger our exposition becomes when we allow the Bible to be in the driver's seat and we learn to sing to the theme tune.

14

Make the Application

THERE CAN BE LITTLE DOUBT that a vital part of any expository talk is applying the biblical text to the listeners' lives. Sometimes preachers suggest that such application is unnecessary; they argue that the work of applying the truth is the prerogative and responsibility of the Holy Spirit, which we should not usurp. It is true, of course, that we cannot convert anyone or produce radical, lasting change in any of our hearers. That is the work of the Holy Spirit alone. Speaking of his own apostolic ministry, Paul told the Corinthians, "Not that we are sufficient in ourselves to claim anything as coming from us, but our sufficiency is from God, who has made us sufficient to be ministers of a new covenant, not of the letter but of the Spirit" (2 Cor. 3:5–6). But there is no conflict between competent ministry and the sovereign authority of the Spirit. The human ingredient is only possible by the power of God's Spirit.

While we must never rely on an unjustified confidence in our own abilities, nevertheless we must remember that God graciously uses human agency to do his work, to be channels of his power. Otherwise, there would be no need for preaching at all. God has instituted a teaching ministry in the church and commanded the preaching of the gospel to the world—and where he commissions, he equips and enables. The Holy Spirit's ministry is to come alongside God's servants as our helper or enabler in order that our service of Christ may be competent (John 14:16–17). The apostolic examples, in both the teaching and writing of the New Testament clearly show that applying the truth to life was a mark of that competence and indeed a major purpose of their ministry. They were the human agents chosen by God from the beginning to do this (see Matt. 28:18–20), and this was the charge given to the next generation, such as Timothy and Titus, as it has been to all others ever since.

Preaching, then, is never simply a matter of conveying information. That may be achieved by a lecture. Preaching is far more relational. As noted earlier, the Spirit of God takes the word of God and relates it through the mind (changing our thinking), to the heart (affecting our personal priorities) in order to activate the will so that Scripture transforms the whole person in thought, word, and action. That is the end goal of application. So when we speak about "making the application," this does not imply that it is the mere invention of the preacher. Rather, we want to identify the practical life implications inherent in a proper understanding of the biblical text and then intentionally explain and relate them to our situation today.

I like to call the application the "transformational intention" of the original author and his text. The expectation built into this sort of application is that God's word properly understood will produce life-changing effects in the lives of its hearers. I have written about this in more detail elsewhere,[1] but its essence is to ask what the biblical author was expecting to happen as a result of the text he was writing. To understand as much as possible the transformational intention of the text will enable me to bring that aim to the very different life contexts of my hearers today—but also with recognition of the unchanging truth that the passage is teaching.

We need to give much prayer, thought, and spiritual wisdom to the application of our preaching, because Scripture warns us that we are

---

1   See esp. chap. 4 in David Jackman, *Transforming Preaching: Reflecting on 50 Years of Word Ministry* (Fearn, Scotland: Christian Focus, 2021).

most vulnerable and often most resistant at the point of putting the truth into practice. All of us, as sinners, have an innate ability to avoid the challenging content of the word. We become adept at taking evasive action or screening out the truth by doing nothing. In Hebrews 3:7–11, the writer uses Psalm 95:7–11 as a warning to his readers about the danger of hardening the heart:

Therefore, as the Holy Spirit says [the implication is that he is still saying it],

"Today, if you hear his voice,
do not harden your hearts." (Heb. 3:7–8)

Clearly, that is the danger every time God's voice is heard, because hardening one's heart against God's word is the default position of sinful human beings. That is where the unseen battle is fought as every sermon is given. Will God's truth be received with life-changing effect, or will it be rejected? To reject it, all I need to do is listen and then do nothing about it, and my sinful heart will harden quite naturally. Preachers need the Spirit's wisdom and the divine gift of perseverance—first to put the "transformational intention" to work in their own lives and then to get past the defense systems that their hearers have set up around their hearts.

An Unhelpful Approach: "Bolt-On" Applications

Sometimes, to try to get past their listeners' defenses, preachers resort to what I call "bolt-on" applications. "Bolt-ons" are popular in our contemporary culture. If you need more capacity on your computer, just pay and add a bolt-on. If you need extra insurance coverage, you can usually bolt it on to your existing policy. A "bolt-on" is an accessory as easily attached as if you could add it with a bolt or nail. It is tempting for preachers to revert to bolt-on applications because they can be attached to a wide variety of texts, saving time and effort. They are usually generalized and nonspecific but will appear to connect powerfully with the hearers. There are two main types of bolt-on application.

1. *"We ought to . . . "* This kind of application uses aspects of Christian discipleship that are unquestionably valid and important, but it turns them into legalistic demands, often presented in the form of unanswerable rhetorical questions. "We ought to" applications are conveyed by guilt-inducing enquiries: "Are you reading the Bible enough, praying enough, giving to the church and missions enough, witnessing enough?" No one is ever going to put up his or her hand and say, "Well, actually, I am!" Everyone is made to feel guilty in a general "I ought to be a better Christian" kind of way. Sadly, the preacher will be tempted to think he has connected with his hearers, when all he has achieved with these repeated generalizations is, on the one hand, an increase of guilt or despair in the sensitive listener or, on the other hand, a failure to challenge and soften the heart of the more obstinate.

2. *"Don't you feel like . . . ?"* This equally popular bolt-on application is often a well-meaning attempt to build a connection between the preacher and the hearers. But it relies on the preacher's imaginative empathy rather than on the intention of the text: "Do you often feel low, discouraged, frustrated, defeated? (I know I do!) Then this is the message for you." But what follows often bears little relationship to the purpose and transformational intention of the text in its contexts.

Bolt-on applications can appear very stirring at the point of delivery, but actually they are subject to the law of diminishing returns because they rely on human ingenuity and imposition, rather than on the Spirit's interpretation and exposition. Even if the application is faithful to Scripture as a whole, if it is ultimately built on what is *not* said in this text, it will lack authority and power.

Determining Application

The challenge for the preacher is how to teach and apply the text in such a way that it accomplishes the purposes for which God inspired it to be written. As we try to stay on the line, listen carefully to the text, set the text in its context, be a time traveler, and sing to the theme tune, we also need to ask the Lord for the skill to make the application. What follows are six priorities to help equip us for this part of our task.

1. Application Is Built into Scripture

The word "therefore" occurs many times in the Bible, often to point out the practical application of particular truths. An obvious example is Romans 8:1: "There is therefore now no condemnation for those who are in Christ Jesus." In Romans 7, Paul has been expounding the fact that his Christian experience involves a struggle between his inner being, which delights in the law of God, and his sinful nature, which inclines him toward evil. This is a battle that our new nature often seems to lose, but as Paul has expounded in the letter, the profound truth of justification is to be balanced against these losses. Through Christ, there is now "no condemnation."

The transformational intention is that we rejoice in our right standing before God with the confidence that this depends entirely on God's justifying grace through Christ's atoning sacrifice, not on our own estimate of our sanctification. In the end, though we stumble and fall on the way, we shall be triumphant because we are in Christ Jesus who has paid the penalty in full so that we cannot be condemned. Including application in their teaching is common among biblical authors, and it needs to be common among preachers as well. Think of all the linking words that biblical authors use—*so, then, but, therefore*—and then look at your sermon notes to see how often such connectors occur in your preaching. Are you linking truth and application, as they do?

2. Application Derives from the Text in Its Context, Not from the Preacher

Context helps us not only to understand the meaning and significance of the text but also to determine its valid application. The discipline of placing the preaching text in its three contexts—the immediate, the book, and the whole Bible contexts—enables us to see how to make the application. Lines of application begin to appear as we move from "them then" to "us now." We need to explain clearly how the application flows from the text so that our hearers understand the implications and are persuaded of their relevance from the text, rather than from our own enthusiasm or ingenuity. Effective preaching happens when the application dawns on the hearers' understanding from the text itself and demands an obedient response. The opposite happens when application is not derived demonstrably from the text but from the preacher. We are not at liberty to introduce application to fulfill our own personal agendas.

3. Application Should Be a Major Concern of the Introduction and Conclusion

Each section of a sermon has its own contribution and significance. But the start and finish are critical, so it is important to give careful thought to both, especially with application in view. The introduction will work best if it focuses on the major application of the talk. The start needs to be crisp and inviting. Make it short, gripping, and relevant in the sense that it introduces the value of the talk for the hearers' lives. An effective approach is to introduce an issue or question that will be addressed or answered by the application.

Make the application the focus of your conclusion too. It's good to end on a note of action. The conclusion should not be overly dramatic but serious, convinced, sincere, and urgent as the transformational intention is pressed home with the help of God's Spirit. Be precise. Give practical examples of a proper response. Don't allow the talk to just fade away. Avoid the temptation to preach the main points over again but use the remaining minutes to root the application in the consciousness of your hearers.

4. Application Connects the Bible's Message to Our World

Careful explanation of the meaning of a Bible text will usually prompt two questions in the minds of the hearers: "So what?" and "How?"

The task of the application is to answer them both, so it is important to think about this during the preparation process—not merely at the end of the preparation. Application must be at the center of our preparation. What is the contemporary take-home value of this text? What should be its impact and implications for life Monday through Saturday, at work and home, with friends and colleagues, in the church and the community?

Preachers often rightly contemplate how to illustrate a particular truth in their exegesis, but our hearers would greatly benefit from illustration of the application. People are helped by specific examples of how the application might look in everyday life. Try to make sure that these application-type illustrations are contemporary ones, with which everyone can easily identify. The ability to picture oneself in a similar real-life situation can be a powerful motivation to action. How should I respond in a situation of temptation or failure when I feel overwhelmed by difficulties or paralyzed by fear? Construct an illustration that puts the hearer in the relevant position and then take them through the stages by which to deal with it according to the exposition of the text.

5. Application Needs to Be Relational to Our Hearers

As we study a text, we may become aware, sometimes quite painfully, of our own excuses for not applying a text to our lives. We need to deal with these for our own spiritual health, but we should also consider our excuses as likely representative of our hearers' reactions to the text. Effective application depends on the preacher coming alongside his hearers. Dealing with our own objections and hesitations will enable us to help our listeners deal with them too. Show that you understand and empathize with these negative reactions. Be sensitive and gracious towards their situations and problems. Assure them that you are on their side (as, indeed, God is) in their struggle to respond in obedience. Don't be aloof or judgmental, as though you have all the problems solved. Rather, share something of your own heart and how the Lord has been dealing with you in these matters.

You can also find helpful examples in Christian biographies. Above all, be relational to the real life circumstances of your congregation and make sure that the applications connect to them where they are.

6. Application Takes Us to Christ as the Center of All the Scriptures

All of God's promises and purposes in Scripture come to their fruition and fulfillment in the Lord Jesus. Our application exalts and glorifies him when it shows how dependent we are on him for the outworking of God's living word in our lives. When God's truth convicts us of our sin, application sends us to Christ who has carried the guilt and penalty for all who repent and believe. When we are made aware of our weakness and inability, application drives us to Christ, in whom are found all the treasures of wisdom and knowledge through his Holy Spirit. When we look to the future, application shows that our hope and perseverance are grounded in the person and work of the Lord Jesus, the King of kings and Lord of lords, now and forever.

We want to make sure our application is Christ centered because the transformational power comes only through the life of Christ planted in our souls by the enabling power of the Holy Spirit. If we are Christ centered, we shall be grace focused. The danger, otherwise, is that the application becomes a list of dos and don'ts, rules and regulations that encourage the hearers to try harder but in their own strength rather than in dependence on the Lord. He is the one to whom all the Scriptures point. He is the supreme and sufficient answer and remedy for every problem. He has the power for every inadequacy. He is the Lord of the universe, the sure and certain refuge, the support and comfort of his people, the one who is full of truth and grace. All our applications should ultimately point our hearers to Christ.

Practical Examples

To better grasp these priorities of faithful application let's look at some practical examples, both positive and negative.

Judges 6:36–40

In this narrative, Gideon, who has been commissioned by God to deliver Israel from the Midianites, asks God to confirm his promise by causing dew to form on a fleece of wool while the ground remains dry (Judg. 6:36–37). God answers, and the next morning Gideon squeezes a bowlful of water from the fleece (Judg. 6:38). But then he asks for the reverse: dew on the ground and dry fleece (Judg. 6:39). This God also grants (Judg. 6:40).

A deficient application would be to jump straight from Gideon to ourselves. After all, he is included in the great cloud of witnesses to faith in Hebrews 11:32. Therefore, we might be encouraged to "lay out a fleece" before God in prayer to discern his will. Another, more fanciful, application would be to challenge the hearers to consider whether their souls are like the dew-enriched fleece or the dry, barren ground. But both of these applications are faulty because they place us in the story and look for points of similarity with our situation. In the first case, we are in charge, deciding what "fleece" we will lay out. But the story depends on the supernatural activity of God, which we cannot command. The second faulty application takes an element of the story and elevates it to a level of interpretation that finds no support in the context.

When we remember that God is the hero of the Old Testament narrative, our application is better centered on what Scripture teaches us about God through the story. The text reveals a gracious God who accommodates himself to Gideon's weak faith to build him up for the challenges ahead. Historical context is significant here, as this comment by Tim Keller shows:

> Gideon was very specifically asking God to show him that he was not one of the forces of nature (like the other gods), but was sovereign over the forces of nature. Gideon, then, was not looking for

"little signs" to help him make a decision. He was really seeking to understand the nature of God. . . . Gideon's request was for help to build up his faith. God, in his grace, responded (twice!).[2]

This is not only faithful to the text but also a helpful encouragement. When we find ourselves fearful or doubtful, we can ask for God's gracious help to overcome our unbelief as we trust in the Lord Jesus in whom "all the promises of God find their Yes" (2 Cor. 1:20).

Luke 5:1–11

This story of the miraculous catch of fish describes the call to discipleship of Peter, James, and John. After a night of fishing that yielded nothing, the fishermen "put out into the deep and let down [their] nets" at Jesus's word (Luke 5:4), and the resulting catch threatens to sink two boats. Peter's response, "Depart from me, for I am a sinful man, O Lord" (Luke 5:8), is met by Jesus's promise, "From now on you will be catching men" (5:10).

Misguided examples of applications might include, "Like the disciples, we need to 'put out into the deep,' to venture beyond our comfort zones, if we are to be successful fishers of people." Or perhaps, "If you 'lend your boat' to Jesus, as Simon Peter did, he will reward you beyond your wildest dreams." But both attempts have the same weakness: a detail from the narrative is spiritualized into a life lesson for us. And the choice of detail from the story is entirely arbitrary, leaving the major thrust and purposes of the narrative in its context virtually untouched.

A better way is to focus application on the Lord Jesus—not on Peter or ourselves. Jesus sovereignly demonstrates his authority in the domain where Peter was the expert. The experienced fisherman acts on Jesus's word, and the miraculous catch follows. So the narrative has lessons about the sovereign authority of Jesus, exercised through his word and

---

2   Timothy Keller, *Judges for You* (Epsom, UK: The Good Book Company, 2013), 78–79.

experienced by obedient, humble submission. Peter realizes how utterly different Jesus is from everyone else. Peter recognizes his sin, confesses Christ as Lord, and receives a life-transforming commission. However, the danger is either to think that we have to replicate Peter or that we are so unlike him that the story has minimal relevance for us. The overflowing nets and call of Peter are wonderful ingredients in the text, but they are unique to this narrative. Yet, the principle of Christ's power and authority over the natural world and the lives of human beings remains true today and challenges us to live under his liberating rule.

1 Corinthians 10:13

This verse comes as the climax of a series of examples from the history of Israel (see 1 Cor. 10:1–12). Paul writes, "No temptation has overtaken you that is not common to man. God is faithful, and he will not let you be tempted beyond your ability, but with the temptation he will also provide the way of escape, that you may be able to endure it" (1 Cor. 10:13). Several applications might be suggested, each containing elements of truth. For example, "Don't think you are a special case when you undergo temptation. Everybody is tempted, but God will see you through." Or perhaps, "Don't be discouraged when you face temptation. The Lord knows how much you can take. He won't allow you to sink under it." Or again, "Don't be careless about temptation. There is always a door marked 'Exit' through God's faithfulness, but you have to use it." How do we choose?

Through this chapter, we have seen that context provides application, and that seems to me to be the conditioning factor here. The first two examples of applications interpret the verse as being primarily a message of comfort and encouragement. That message is certainly present. Trust a faithful God who will not let you be overwhelmed by testing but will provide the way of escape. However, the context shows that the emphatic note is one of warning. The preceding verse makes this plain, "Let anyone who thinks that he stands, take heed lest he fall"

(1 Cor. 10:12), as does the following verse, "Therefore, my beloved, flee from idolatry" (10:14). Thus, the point of 10:13 is not that we all experience temptation but, rather, that we may be lulled into a false confidence that we are immune to sins that are "common to man."

In the wider context (1 Cor. 10:6–11), Paul has been listing such sins in the history of Israel: idolatry (10:7), sexual immorality (10:8), testing God (10:9), and grumbling (10:10). In committing these sins in the wilderness, they have become examples (1 Cor. 10:6, 11), warning us not to desire evil as they did. These remain sins common to humanity, and they still defile Christian lives and church communities today. According to 1 Corinthians 10:13, in the faithfulness of God the way of escape is always open, but we have to avail ourselves of it by fleeing from temptation. There is encouragement and assurance here, but the predominant aspect of application is warning.

This work on application matters because the overarching aim of the Bible is to bring us to know God personally through Jesus Christ (see John 17:3; 20:31). This is so that we may grow into his likeness (see Acts 20:32; Phil. 3:8–11; Col. 1:9–10; 2 Pet. 3:18) as he restores his own image in his redeemed people (see 2 Cor. 3:18). Each passage of Scripture leads us to a personal, relational knowledge of God, the holy Trinity. So wherever we encounter God, we encounter Jesus.

We are to love God with our whole being (see Deut. 6:5; Matt. 22:37–40), which means responding to his divine self-revelation in the Lord Jesus Christ, the Word made flesh. Loving God means believing in Christ, receiving his word, obeying his instruction, and following him. So biblical exposition will always take us to the glories of who Christ is and the wonders of what he has done for us by using the uniqueness of each text to exalt Christ—to demonstrate something of his person and work—and so motivate us to love and follow him. Our applications will then be grace driven, since we know that we can never grow in our likeness to Christ unless he is actively transforming us from the inside out through the dynamic of his indwelling Holy Spirit.

We need to remember that the Bible is God's book about himself before it is his book about us. Our natural inclination is to concentrate on ourselves, but that is not the primary focus of revelation. Every passage of Scripture needs to be viewed through the lens of the person and work of the Lord Jesus. He surpasses all the godly examples of Bible characters. He transcends the categories of prophet, priest, king, wise man, temple, sacrifice, and so on. However, we should not use the Old Testament merely as a springboard to get to the gospel by the quickest route. We must let each passage speak with its own authentic tone and content and then apply the interpretation lens of Christ by considering what difference it makes that Christ has now come. Christ-centered application does not try to discover where he is "hiding" in every verse. Nor do we need to impose Christ on the text. Rather, we must recognize how a particular passage, within the sweep of the whole Bible metanarrative, distinctively points to Christ and what our proper response to him should be.

15

Beware Framework

WHEN WE SET OURSELVES to understand or interpret any text, biblical or not, we are unable to approach it without certain preconceived ideas and convictions. We bring our presuppositions, our theological worldview, and our personal experience to the text. We would be naïve to think otherwise. These constitute our framework, our grid, our set of principles and points of reference that we use when we form decisions and judgments. This framework is personal and unique to each one of us, shaped by our background and upbringing, our Christian history, the issues occupying our secular culture, and so on. Our framework will therefore dictate how we approach, interpret, and preach a text, often without us even realizing it. It is the lens through which we view any and every text. But the danger for the preacher is that the framework usurps the driver's seat that should be occupied by the text so that the word of God is conditioned and governed by the thoughts of man. That is why we must beware framework.

Advantages and Disadvantages of Framework

Of course, our framework carries with it certain advantages. It will reflect our personal and contemporary cultural values, which may help us to connect with our hearers. It helps us to organize our thoughts and enquiries on the basis of convictions we have already worked through and made our own. It provides a reference point of certainty when we are seeking to evaluate new ideas or speculative interpretations. As we compare Scripture with Scripture, we use our framework to interpret a specific text against the background of what we have come to accept as the Bible's clear teaching on similar themes or issues.

Nevertheless, the danger remains that we may uncritically seek to fit every text into our framework so that it becomes our main interpretative tool. In such situations, we may become lazy about our preparation so that instead of the hard work of exegesis and analysis, we are tempted simply to relate the text to a familiar idea in our framework. That will mean, in turn, that we do not learn anything new nor are we stimulated in our study by fresh discoveries. If we become addicted to short cuts in our preparation, it will not be long before our preached material is stale or becomes muddled. A framework easily takes over and drowns the text. Frameworks become familiar to our hearers and are soon screened out as predictable and boring.

When under pressure of time, many of us have no doubt resorted to preaching our framework. Familiar Bible words occur in the text—such as grace, hope, sin, or repentance—so we unload from our framework memory bank the familiar thinking that the words trigger for us. Accompanied by cross references, favorite illustrations, and exhortations, the sermon has been created, but in fact the text has been accommodated to our framework. For some preachers a particular doctrine or theological emphasis can become so dominant that it surfaces at some point in every sermon. What is preached may well be true and even helpful, but it is not the primary message of the text and the end result is the speaker's agenda, rather than the word of God.

The preaching of one's own agenda can appear an attractive option to a local church pastor who is rightly seeking to bring about development and growth in his congregation. He may wish to mobilize the congregation to evangelism, or to plant new churches, or to engage in community outreach. All these are laudable objectives. But when the agenda takes over the preaching, the framework rules the message, and the connections to the text become increasingly tenuous. In the end, the preacher's framework has been imposed on the text, and he has forfeited the authority of the word and the Spirit.

Because we each inevitably have a framework, we must ensure that it serves our expository purpose and does not replace it. If we fit a text into our existing framework, we are in danger of obscuring or nullifying the unique message of Scripture. As a guard against framework-dominance, we need to make sure that our exegesis of a particular text prompts us to ask questions of the framework. We want our framework to be challenged, reduced, or developed by our deepening encounter with the true and living God in his active and powerful word. As our framework is regularly critiqued by Scripture, it will become less likely to assert itself and more aligned with the priorities of the word.

Being conscious of our biases can help us to reshape them where necessary. It can be beneficial to ask others who hear us regularly to watch for times when we resort to preaching our framework. When preparing to preach a text, we should cultivate the discipline of comparing other biblical passages that deal with parallel themes so that we can amend both our interpretation and our framework accordingly. This is the value of reading widely in commentaries or listening to quality expository talks so that we may broaden our understanding of the issues involved and the ways that other preachers approach them. In doing so, we will come to firmer convictions on a wide variety of subjects and ensure that our framework becomes increasingly biblical.

Examples

As an exercise in learning to beware our assumed framework, let us examine five example biblical texts. To ensure that the word remains in the driver's seat and that our framework is subservient to it, we will answer a set of four diagnostic questions with each text:

- To whom is the text addressed, and how does that connect to our hearers?
- Do the words and phrases of the text have the same meanings as those presupposed by the assumed framework?
- What is the original purpose of the text, and is that purpose reflected in the assumed framework?
- Does the text fit in the assumed framework, or is it primarily about something else?

Isaiah 30:21

We begin with a well-known promise from Isaiah that is often assumed to speak of obtaining personal guidance from the Lord: "And your ears shall hear a word behind you, saying, 'This is the way, walk in it,' when you turn to the right or when you turn to the left" (Isa. 30:21). Your framework may include some strong convictions about God's guidance, including your own experience of God's providence in your life circumstances. It might seem convenient to use the verse to encourage the congregation that God has a plan for each of them and that he is overseeing the direction of their lives. The verse fits into a supposed framework in which clear and specific instruction will be forthcoming from the Lord to help them make difficult decisions. But we must ask ourselves whether the verse actually teaches this. The text needs to question the framework, which can be done by answering a series of four questions to provide clarity.

To whom is the text addressed, and how does that connect to our hearers? To whom does the repeated "you" refer in the verse? Clearly, it refers to the people of God during the reign of Hezekiah, who are under threat of invasion because of their unfaithfulness and refusal to heed God's word. Yet, in spite of this, Isaiah prophesies that their affliction will end and God will show them his grace—though they do not deserve it. This connects to us and our hearers, since both God's grace and discipline are operative towards his new covenant people, even though we too often fail him and prove unfaithful.

Do the words and phrases of the text have the same meanings as those presupposed by the assumed framework? What does "turn to the right or . . . turn to the left" signify? In the context, it is not a choice between two paths, as in the supposed framework suggested above. Instead, turning to the right or left represents the ever-present danger of leaving God's way entirely. This is what the people of Judah in Isaiah's day had done by rejecting God's word, but God promises a better future.

What is the original purpose of the text, and is that purpose reflected in the assumed framework? The nation had largely rejected God's word, but Isaiah reveals that a time is coming when they will hear and listen to God's voice telling them how they should live. Through his instruction the Lord will provide watchful care over them to preserve them in the way of faith.

Does the text fit in the assumed framework, or is it primarily about something else? The verse does not address how individuals obtain personal guidance from the Lord for difficult decisions. Actually, it applies to the whole community. The text promises that God will call his people back to wholehearted loyalty and covenant obedience not by an audible voice but by his spoken/written word. This is how he will preserve his people. Grounded in what God promises, we can assure our hearers that God is always at work, preserving and protecting us so that his people stand firm in faith and reject false gods.

1 Corinthians 2:2

Another verse that a preacher's framework might be tempted to appropriate for prooftext purposes is 1 Corinthians 2:2. Paul writes, "For I decided to know nothing among you except Jesus Christ and him crucified." It is sometimes claimed that, after the comparatively limited response to Paul's speech to the philosophers in Athens in which he deconstructed their worldview (Acts 17:22–34), he moved on to Corinth (Acts 18:1) with a determination in the future to preach only the simple gospel of the cross without any specific cultural contextualization. This framework is then used to claim that dialogue with the cultural presuppositions of our hearers may obscure and even hinder the reception of the gospel. But is that what the verse is saying? We need to ask our four diagnostic questions.

To whom is the text addressed, and how does that connect to our hearers? It is clear that Paul is addressing the Corinthian believers but not as a direct instruction to them about ministry content. Rather, he is giving them a historical reminder of the heart of the message that gave birth to the church and that some seem to have forgotten.

Do the words and phrases of the text have the same meanings as those presupposed by the assumed framework? The framework outlined above can unhelpfully lead us to limit the word "know" to mean "preach." But Paul's concern is wider than initial gospel preaching. For Paul, the cross is not only the way into Christian experience but also its distinctive hallmark. The central truth needed to produce and shape Christian growth and spirituality is to know Christ and him crucified.

What is the original purpose of the text, and is that purpose reflected in the assumed framework? A false set of spiritual values had developed in the Corinthian church. Some were so keen to win the approval of their secular fellow citizens that they were moving from the wisdom and power of Christ crucified to a more culturally comfortable and seemingly persuasive version of the faith. They were looking for miraculous signs and impressive oratorical performances. Therefore, Paul reminds them that the church in Corinth came into existence not through human wisdom or ability but in the demonstration of divine power through the proclamation of a crucified Messiah.

Does the text fit in the assumed framework, or is it primarily about something else? First Corinthians 2:1 tells us that Paul had rejected "lofty speech or wisdom"—which is what the Corinthians were enticed by and looking for—in favor of the message of the cross. Moreover, he hadn't used "lofty speech or wisdom" in Athens either. In fact, he was labeled by the intellectuals there as a "babbler" (Acts 17:18). Thus, Paul isn't thinking about Athens but addressing the situation in Corinth. The Corinthians wanted impressive shows of worldly wisdom, so he reminds them that they are only Christians through knowing Christ crucified. First Corinthians 2:2 does not rule out a place for apologetics. Rather, Paul's point is that the gospel that saved them does not rely on the ability of the messenger but on the content of the message itself. Their focus should be on the cross and, therefore, on the person of Christ, rather than on the preacher.

2 Timothy 2:2

After exhorting Timothy to be strengthened by Christ's grace (2 Tim. 2:1), Paul continues, "What you have heard from me in the presence of many witnesses entrust to faithful men, who will be able to teach others also" (2:2). For many preachers, their framework includes strong convictions about the need for more Christians to be involved in the ministry of the gospel—in evangelism, pastoral care, teaching, and so on. This verse fits into such a framework as a means of stirring up lethargic hearers to greater efforts. But is that what Paul is addressing?

To whom is the text addressed, and how does that connect to our hearers? Is everyone to be so entrusted? The "you" in the text is Timothy, the pastor-teacher in Ephesus, who is to entrust ministry to men who are "faithful" and "able to teach." This is a specific instruction to Timothy to look for qualified men to shoulder the task of ministry—not those who are academically clever or who possess magnetic personalities but those who are qualified through consistent godly living and ability to teach the word. Not everyone fits these qualifications.

Do the words and phrases of the text have the same meanings as those presupposed by the assumed framework? The verb "entrust" is significant. Paul describes his commission to guard the gospel as a sacred trust from God; now as Paul's departure draws near, Timothy must accept the same obligation (2 Tim. 1:12–14) and see that it is passed on faithfully to qualified teachers (2:2). Paul's concern, then, is for the preservation

of the apostolic gospel and teaching, which is not a ministry requirement of every member.

*What is the original purpose of the text, and is that purpose reflected in the
assumed framework?* Paul's purpose is not to stir up lethargic hearers to
greater efforts but to exhort and remind Timothy about the content of his
ministry—the apostolic teaching that he had often witnessed Paul proclaim
in public. There must be no deviation from the line of truth, whether by
Timothy or by those whom he will entrust with this ministry task.

*Does the text fit in the assumed framework, or is it primarily about
something else?* A framework focused too narrowly on equipping believers for ministry could easily lead one to miss the central emphasis
of 2 Timothy 2:2. Paul is concerned for the preservation and proclamation of the true gospel, which should be our concern too. The
assumed framework should not lead us to apply this text to everyone;
the strongest and most direct application is to preachers. We have to
ensure that we are guarding the good deposit of the gospel and also
passing it on to a new cohort of teachers, who will themselves raise up
others. A major part of ministry work is to equip and qualify others
to preach and teach the word faithfully. That is the continuing burden
of this verse for us today.

Philippians 4:13

Paul writes, "I can do all things through him who strengthens me" (Phil.
4:13). This is a popular verse that a preacher's framework may lead him
to use to encourage Christians to take on some new form of service.
Church members may assume that they are incapable of certain kinds
of ministry, like teaching Sunday School or engaging in door-to-door
evangelism, but in the Lord's strength, according to Philippians 4:13,
they can do it. After all, Paul says they can do "all things." But is that
really what he means? The biblical text needs to question the framework.

To whom is the text addressed, and how does that connect to our hearers?
The Philippian Christians have been in generous partnership with Paul

in his gospel work. They continue to be concerned for him in prison (Phil. 1:13), but they have had no opportunity to give until now (4:10). In the assumed framework, Paul's specific personal testimony is used to encourage Christians to attempt any form of service, irrespective of gift, ability, or aptitude.

Do the words and phrases of the text have the same meanings as those presupposed by the assumed framework? The phrase "all things" relates primarily to the variety of financial situations Paul had experienced during his ministry, characterized in Philippians 4:12 as both "abundance and need." He has "learned in whatever situation . . . to be content" (Phil. 4:11), and this unshakeable contentment has come "through him who strengthens me" (4:13).

What is the original purpose of the text, and is that purpose reflected in the assumed framework? Paul's purpose is to set his readers' minds at ease about his needs, since he is writing from prison. In the verses that follow (Phil. 4:14–20), he recounts their past generosity with great thankfulness, including a recent visit from their representative Epaphroditus, who carried a sacrificial gift from them (Phil. 4:18). Yet his concern is not with the provision for his own welfare, but for "the fruit that increases to your credit" (Phil. 4:17). The Philippians will experience God meeting their needs, as Paul has through them (Phil. 4:19). This is the apostle's personal testimony from his own experience.

Does the text fit in the assumed framework, or is it primarily about something else? It is true, of course, that Christ is the ultimate provider for his people, whatever our circumstances, and we can rely on him to provide us with his divine strength so that we too can be content. But if a preacher uses the text to stimulate the congregation to serve in any area—no matter what their gifts and abilities—the text has become lost in the preacher's framework. Instead, we need to be encouraged by knowing and trusting that God will strengthen us to meet all circumstances with contentment. As Alec Motyer writes, "It is finally because of Christ that Paul is contented, and it is Christ whom he offers to us as the means and guarantee of our contentment. For Paul, the person who possesses Christ possesses all."[1]

Exodus 19:4–6

In this passage, God instructs Moses on Mount Sinai about what to tell the people of Israel:

> You yourselves have seen what I did to the Egyptians, and how I bore you on eagles' wings and brought you to myself. Now therefore, if you will indeed obey my voice and keep my covenant, you shall be my treasured possession among all peoples, for all the earth is mine; and you shall be to me a kingdom of priests and a holy nation. (Ex. 19:4–6)

One's framework might suggest that this verse presents an opportunity to stress the importance of obedience. Since Jesus himself said, "If you love me, you will keep my commandments" (John 14:15), we should call our hearers to make stronger efforts to obey Christ, as Israel was challenged to keep the law covenant. Is this what Exodus 19:4–6 is communicating?

To whom is the text addressed, and how does that connect to our hearers? God is speaking through Moses to the people of Israel who had just arrived at Sinai three months after God rescued them from slavery in Egypt. On the night before the exodus, they had been delivered from God's judgment on the firstborn by placing their faith in his sacrificial provision of the Passover lamb. The blood of the lambs on their doorposts was a sign of their trust and obedience. That is to be the pattern of their future life, as it is of God's new covenant people—through the sacrificial death of "Christ, our Passover lamb" (1 Cor. 5:7).

Do the words and phrases of the text have the same meanings as those presupposed by the assumed framework? In this text the meaning of the

---

1   J. Alec Motyer, *The Message of Philippians*, The Bible Speaks Today (Nottingham, UK: Inter-Varsity Press, 1984), 221.

vocabulary is accessible to the ordinary reader and does not require any special interpretation.

What is the original purpose of the text, and is that purpose reflected in the assumed framework? These verses provide significant revelation about God's character and purposes, revelation that preceded the giving of the law (Ex. 20–23), which was itself the expression of God's character and will. These verses, however, are rooted in grace, not law. Israel's salvation from Egypt was entirely the Lord's work (19:4). They were rescued in faithful fulfillment of his promises to Abraham. Moreover, this rescue was relational. As the Lord testified, "I . . . brought you to myself" (19:4) not just to Sinai. Their future obedience to the law was the condition by which the channel of grace would be kept open so that they could enjoy and experience all that God had planned for them in their relationship with him as his "treasured possession" (19:5). However, the relationship was not established by their obedience; it had already been established by God's sovereign grace. He did not first give the law and then deliver the people. On the contrary, he delivered the people and then gave them the law. This explains why in Exodus 20:1–2, before the giving of the Ten Commandments, God reminds them that he brought them out of the house of slavery. Grace before law is the pattern. So obedience to the law demonstrates the love and loyalty of covenant people for their covenant Lord. It was never intended to be the means by which that relationship was established. The wrong framework emphasis could easily obscure the main intention of the text.

Does the text fit in the assumed framework, or is it primarily about something else? The danger is that we might focus on and stress only the law aspect of the text and completely miss the grace emphasis. Of course, as Jesus taught us, obedience to his commands is supremely important. But this text is about both grace and law. In fact, the law ingredient only makes sense when we have understood grace. Otherwise, two wrong emphases can occur. First, if we focus only on the law aspect, we can imply that Old Testament people were saved by the law, while we are saved by grace. Second, if we do not maintain the text's emphasis on grace, we may end up subtly hinting that law keeping is a means of earning acceptance with God. It is then a short step to add on extra biblical rules and regulations from our Christian subculture, as a condition for experiencing God's grace and winning his approval. This was Paul's concern in his letter to the Galatians as he explained how destructive this error is: "You are severed from Christ, you who would be justified by the law; you have fallen away from grace" (Gal. 5:4). Richard L. Pratt summarizes this helpfully when he writes,

> Put simply, Old Testament theocratic Law was designed to glorify God and to benefit Israel. It separated the theocracy from other nations and made Israel God's "treasured possession." The Law of Moses taught Israel how to please and honor God. Moreover, it protected Israel from sin's destructive power and pointed to the way of fruitful living (Joshua 1:7–8). Through the course of time, sin turned the Law into a heavy burden (Romans 7:7–11), but God's expressed purpose in giving the Law was to bless his people.[2]

So beware framework! It is an inevitable factor in our study of every text, but we must not allow it to dictate the meaning of the text uncritically. We must seek consciously to amend our framework in light of what we learn from Scripture every time we preach. Let the text question the framework so that our understanding of both may be deepened and enriched by the experience.

---

2   Richard L. Pratt Jr., *He Gave Us Stories: The Bible Student's Guide to Interpreting Old Testament Narratives* (Phillipsburg, NJ: P&R,1990), 370.

16

Echo the Bible's Tone

SINCE GOD IS the perfect communicator, his word is not only infallible in its content but also provides us with his perfect model for our communication. The Bible contains a wide range of emotions, expressed by God and by its human authors. Because we are made in God's image and likeness, our emotions and affections are a reflection of God's own mind and heart. So we should not be surprised that the breadth and depth of human experience is represented in the Scriptures and that many different tones are employed by the Spirit to convey the truth and apply its impact to the human heart.

In chapter 2, we considered Phillips Brooks's description of preaching as "the bringing of truth through personality."[1] That is both a wonderful possibility and a subtle danger. If we are to convey biblical truth faithfully, we must do so with the Bible's tone, since the content and the manner of the text are intricately woven together and must not be separated. We want our preaching to emulate the Bible's tone so that what we say and how we say it is a channel of God's word.

The tone of our preaching is much more than a matter of volume or gestures. We do need to give attention to the pitch and variety of

1 Phillips Brooks, *Lectures on Preaching: Delivered before the Divinity School of Yale College in January and February, 1877* (New York: E. P. Dutton & Company, 1907), 5.

our voice. We should be thoughtful about the pace of our presentation. Deliberate contrasts of speed with the judicious use of pauses can help make the message more accessible to our hearers. But when the preacher's own tone dominates the sermon, it will have an intrusive, grating effect. A congregation knows when the preacher is working himself up by shouting or dramatic body language, and they begin to regard such theatricality for what it is—mere entertainment or emotional manipulation. Similarly, they know when a preacher is trying to ingratiate himself with them by telling a series of jokes or funny stories, turning himself into a sort of stand-up comedian. They are no longer sitting under God's word but evaluating a human performance.

The words of John the Baptist, the great herald of the Lord Jesus, are appropriate for every preacher to adopt as both a model and a prayer: "He must increase, but I must decrease" (John 3:30). Our desire must be to see Christ exalted and ourselves hidden. Our aim should not merely be to preach well (though we should set the highest standards for ourselves); our supreme aim should be to glorify God. And it is a fact that you cannot bring glory to God and draw attention to yourself at the same time. We are handling his word of eternal truth, which is an awesome responsibility, so we must strive to accurately replicate the Bible's tone in our proclamation.

Biblical Tones

Echoing the Bible's tone is not about putting on a special voice or producing certain emotional responses. It can only be achieved by entering into the heart concerns of the original writer as he was inspired by the Holy Spirit and allowing the text's meaning and significance to penetrate our minds and hearts so that we speak it as God does. The more deeply it stirs our affections, the more powerfully it will affect our hearers through us. This attitude of heart will determine how faithfully we echo the Bible's tone. Let's look at some examples of different tones expressed in the Bible that will help us develop this aspect of our preaching.

Tender Plea

In many places in Scripture there is a tender pleading on the part of God, who is love (1 John 4:8), even in a context of judgement. This is because he "desires all people to be saved and to come to the knowledge of the truth" (1 Tim. 2:4). For example, in the midst of strong statements about the inevitability of God's judgment against his people's rebellion, the prophet Ezekiel speaks for God, who tenderly pleads, "Cast away from you all the transgressions that you have committed, and make yourselves a new heart and a new spirit! Why will you die, O house of Israel? For I have no pleasure in the death of anyone, declares the Lord God; so turn, and live" (Ezek. 18:31–32). You can feel the anguish that motivates the appeal, the heartfelt compassion and tender pleading, the loving logic of the futility of sin. When we are preaching the judgment of God, appealing for repentance, we should do so with anguish in our hearts and tears in our eyes.

Consider also the tenderness of Jesus in the context of his words of judgment: "O Jerusalem, Jerusalem, the city that kills the prophets and stones those who are sent to it! How often would I have gathered your children together as a hen gathers her brood under her wings, and you were not willing!" (Matt. 23:37). Such compassion cannot be fabricated; it is the fruit of genuine love. Notice that the message of judgment is in no way compromised or diluted by this gracious, tender pleading. In fact, it is intensified by the emotions of disappointment and desperate loss. But sometimes contemporary preaching of God's judgment reveals little real love or concern for those being addressed. It is presented either with a matter-of-fact sterility or even as a triumphalist vindication, which is not an echo of the Bible's tone.

Affectionate Rebuke

Paul's letter to the Galatians provides us with a valuable example of how affection and rebuke can be blended. In fact, the rebuke is motivated by the affection. In most of his letters, Paul follows his words of greeting with thanksgiving and appreciation for God's work in the lives of his readers. However, in Galatians he immediately writes, "I am astonished that you are so quickly deserting him who called you in the grace of Christ and are turning to a different gospel" (Gal. 1:6). The situation is serious. If the Galatians are really turning from God to embrace a different gospel, which is no gospel at all, they are in grave danger. The anxiety Paul feels for them expresses itself, not in a tone of white-hot anger, but in bewilderment mixed with loving correction, appealing to them to think about what they are doing. His question, "O foolish Galatians! Who has bewitched you?" (Gal. 3:1), catches the love and frustration in the apostle's heart. Later he writes, "I wish I could be present with you now and change my tone, for I am perplexed about you" (Gal. 4:20). This blend of rebuke and affection will often be needed in our own preaching and in pastoral counsel, when we see dearly loved brothers and sisters being deluded. The measure of its effectiveness will depend on the blend of persuasive teaching of the truth, by logical argument, and personal pastoral affection and concern for those being led astray.

Correcting Irony

There is a place for irony when pastoral love for the Lord's wandering sheep needs to startle them into an awareness of their folly. We might liken this to the ministry of the sheep dog! However, we need to distinguish clearly the difference between irony and sarcasm. There is a bitterness about sarcasm that involves scorn or contempt for the person or object being critiqued. There is no room for that in our preaching. But Paul displays an ironic tone toward the Corinthians when he exposes the empty triumphalism of those who had little time for an apostle who was so unimpressive and who had suffered so much. He writes,

Already you have all you want! Already you have become rich! Without us you have become kings! And would that you did reign, so that we might share the rule with you! . . . We are fools for Christ's sake, but you are wise in Christ. We are weak, but you are strong. You are held in honor, but we in disrepute. (1 Cor. 4:8, 10)

Paul brings the foolishness of their inflated triumphalism home to them by shaming them into realizing the fantasy and hypocrisy of their position. This tone needs to be used with caution and motivated by love, not frustration. Otherwise, it can easily descend into derision, but if used wisely it can be a powerful way of exposing the poverty of thinking and the folly of actions that are governed by secular values rather than God's truth.

Logical Persuasion

It is the logical development and application of apostolic gospel theology that is so persuasive and winsome in the New Testament. There is a strong, coherent flow as the argument moves forward so that as the mind is convinced by the truth being expounded, the application can be made to the whole of life. We need to echo that tone by coming alongside our hearers to explain the content of the argument and then helping them to work out its implications. The tone is that of the empathetic teacher who sits down to explain what one does not yet understand, rather than that of the expert who simply hands down information. This tone is never uncaring, never drily academic, but uses the persuasive logic of God's revealed truth to expose our inadequate thinking and compromised behavior.

This was always the apostolic method. In the synagogue at Thessalonica, where Paul "reasoned with them from the Scriptures, explaining and proving" that Jesus is the Christ, the result was that "some of them were *persuaded*" (Acts 17:2–4). In Corinth, he "reasoned in the synagogue every Sabbath, and tried to *persuade* Jews and Greeks" (Acts 18:4). In Ephesus, he "spoke boldly, reasoning and *persuading* them about the kingdom of God" (Acts 19:8). That same preaching priority is reflected in the letters. Think of how, when writing to the Ephesians, Paul expounds the glories of the gospel for the Gentiles in the first half of the letter and, on that basis, argues for a radically changed lifestyle in the second half. Since God has done so much to bring them into his family, it is profoundly illogical for them to continue living in their pre-Christian lifestyle: "Now this I say and testify in the Lord, that you must no longer walk as the Gentiles do, in the futility of their minds" (Eph. 4:17). Or think how Peter argues that suffering for Christ is a sign of hope and a cause of rejoicing (1 Pet. 4:12–13). It would be illogical to devote a mind and body, which have endured persecution for Jesus's sake, to a life of self-indulgence or compromise with sin (1 Pet. 4:1–3). The tone of logical persuasion is one we must learn to echo.

Penetrating Question

This tone is especially noticeable in Jesus's own teaching. Often he answers a question with a question, or introduces a question that leaves the hearer hanging, or formulates a question that drives straight to the heart of the issue. Think of the conclusion of the parable of the unjust judge, who eventually grants justice to the importunate widow because she wears him out by her persistence. Jesus then says, "Will not God give justice to his elect, who cry to him day and night? Will he delay long over them? I tell you, he will give justice to them speedily. Nevertheless, when the Son of Man comes, will he find faith on earth?" (Luke 18:7–8). God is the polar opposite of the unjust judge. That is the point of the first two questions that Jesus himself answers. But what about that final shocking question? Will Jesus find faith on earth when he returns? With that question the issue becomes much more personal, forcing us to think through the implications. It motivates us to live faithfully, anticipating his return by committing to prayer without losing heart (Luke 18:1).

Jesus often asked insightful, penetrating questions to give his hearers space to think issues through. Think of his encounters with Nicodemus

(John 3:1–15), the Samaritan woman (John 4:7–26), or the lawyer (Luke 10:25–37). When we preach, we may tell ourselves that we must sew up all the arguments in our sermon by relentless pressure. Instead, a questioning tone may get further because it challenges our hearers to think deeply and pursue the implications for themselves.

Solemn Warning

In the teaching of Jesus, solemn warning often runs closely with his tender pleading. For example, the gracious invitation of Matthew 11:28–29, with its appeal to the weary and heavy laden to come to Christ to find rest, is preceded by the solemn warnings of Matthew 11:21–22 against Chorazin and Bethsaida: "For if the mighty works done in you had been done in Tyre and Sidon, they would have repented long ago in sackcloth and ashes. But I tell you, it will be more bearable on the day of judgment for Tyre and Sidon than for you." The warning is uncompromisingly straight: "Woe to you!" (Matt. 11:21). The solemnity is derived from the terrible consequences of their refusal to repent. This makes the tender pleading all the more persuasive in its appeal to turn to Christ while there is still opportunity before the judgment falls. It is no act of love toward our hearers to pass over or muzzle the solemn realities of judgment and hell, when the Lord Jesus himself spoke so often about them. To fail to echo his solemn warning tone is to betray Christ and to consign our hearers to a false hope and a lost eternity.

Joyful Encouragement

There is much in Scripture to encourage us, but we can often miss its exhortations to joyfully exult in who the Lord is and what he has done for us. David writes,

> Oh, magnify the LORD with me,
>> and let us exalt his name together! (Ps. 34:3)

Or again, speaking on God's behalf, he writes,

> Let those who delight in my righteousness
>> shout for joy and be glad
>> and say evermore,
> "Great is the LORD,
>> who delights in the welfare of his servant!" (Ps. 35:27)

You cannot preach passages like this without conveying the joy through the sermon. We may not be used to expressing or able to express our emotions in the way David did, but we must not iron out biblical exhortations like this with a flat, disinterested statement of truth. It is said of some believers that their joy is so deep that it never seems to surface! We must not be among their number. The cause of our rejoicing will always be in the truth we are expounding. But let's not be content with the cause; let's also ask God to help us express it through the way we preach it.

Isaiah provides us with a great example of how to do this as he rejoices in God's forgiving grace of redemption. He writes, speaking for the Lord,

> I have blotted out your transgressions like a cloud
>> and your sins like a mist;
> return to me, for I have redeemed you. (Isa. 44:22)

Isaiah's response involves the whole created order in the joy:

> Sing, O heavens, for the LORD has done it;
>> shout, O depths of the earth;
> break forth into singing, O mountains,
>> O forest, and every tree in it!
> For the LORD has redeemed Jacob,
>> and will be glorified in Israel. (Isa. 44:23)

This joyful encouragement is obviously directed toward the redeemed themselves. If the whole of creation is singing for joy, how can God's people not be leading the celebration? If we need more help to do this together as a congregation, let's learn from and use Psalm 103:1–5 and similar passages to extend our range and deepen our joy.

Practical Guidelines

Wherever a passage stands in the sweep of the whole Bible, we must not only exposit its unique content but also preach it so that our tone aligns with that of the inspired text, using the range of our human emotions. But as we do that, it will be helpful to keep the following practical guidelines in mind.

Don't Be Afraid to Preach the Negatives

We may find that preaching the negatives of Scripture—those messages that people consider offensive—increasingly challenging in a culture that clearly rejects Holy Scripture and asserts its independence from God. Personal freedom is such an idol of our world that the prohibitions of Scripture will often be caricatured as aggressive and demeaning. Our task is to tell the truth, the whole truth, and nothing but the truth—"This is what the Lord says." But preaching the negatives is the necessary precursor to preaching the positives, because they are different sides of the same coin.

You cannot properly preach Jesus's wonderful statement, "I am the way, and the truth, and the life," if you do not also preach the negative, "No one comes to the Father except through me" (John 14:6). The one makes sense of the other. Or think of Jesus's teaching in the Sermon on the Mount where, before urging the practice of almsgiving, prayer, and fasting, he first exposes the Pharisaical hypocrisy of practicing one's righteousness before others in order to be admired by them (Matt. 6:1–18). Sometimes preachers are urged to preach only the positive messages of Scripture because the world around us is so negative and discouraging. But to rightly echo the Bible's tone we must preach its negatives precisely so that we can embrace its positives.

What we must *not* do is develop a negative tone toward our hearers. The attitude of the heart is often revealed in the tone of voice. If the preacher has a negative attitude, it will be apparent in the way he addresses the congregation—criticizing, carping, cajoling. When rebuke is called for, we are to speak the truth in love, because rebuke is always with a view towards repentance and restoration, which is why it can only be preached properly when it is done with compassion and grace.

Don't Equate Your Congregation with the Original Hearers

When preaching the book of Amos, for example, we have to remember that we are not preaching to rebellious eighth-century-BC Israelites. The words addressed to Amos's hearers will of course speak to us today because it is God's living and enduring word, but Amos's hearers are not ours. The content of the message has to be interpreted in the light of Christ's coming, but the tone of Amos's prophecy—whether rebuke, sorrow, or gracious invitation—needs to be reflected in our preaching of the text. We must not equate our hearers with the original recipients. They are not the people of Judah facing the Assyrian invasion or Timothy pastoring in Ephesus. We must remember that the Bible was written *for* us but not directly *to* us. Therefore, we want to help our listeners discern what God is teaching about himself and about us so that the principles come to us from the original context with transforming relevance and power.

Don't Become Hostile toward Your Congregation

When congregations seem not to respond to God's truth, the preacher can be tempted to allow his disappointment to turn into aggression. But we must resist using the law, or our own rules and regulations, to chastise our hearers. The pastor's big stick never produces lasting change; rather we need to seek to win resistant listeners through the grace of the gospel. Avoid the temptation to vent your frustrations on your hearers. Remember how longsuffering, gentle, and patient God is with us and ask him to enable you to echo his tone of steadfast love and kindness.

Don't Be Condescending toward Your Congregation

Some preachers convey the idea that they are treating their hearers like immature children. We all know the difference between unconditional love and the sort of affection that is only given when we are living up to the other person's expectations of us. Congregations instinctively know when a preacher is looking down on them or considers them spiritually inferior. Under such circumstances, hearts will rapidly harden. Remember that the sheep do not belong to the human pastor or leader. As undershepherds called by the chief shepherd, we are to exercise oversight, "not domineering over those in your charge, but being examples to the flock" (1 Pet. 5:3).

The use of a condescending, impatient, or aggressive tone reveals more about the preacher's heart than the needs of his hearers. It shows that the preacher has lost confidence in the vital truth that, if God's word is preached with God's tone, God's Spirit will use it to accomplish his purposes in the lives of those who hear.

Effective preaching not only exegetes the text but also the congregation to whom it is being preached. We must echo the Bible's tone. If we love the people, relate to them, care for them, feed and nurture them, and above all pray for them, our preaching will echo the voice of the good shepherd. Our privilege is to enter into the joys and sorrows of our listeners, to identify with their problems and challenges, to sit where they sit and feel what they are feeling. That quality of empathy will have a deep effect on the tone of our preaching and will produce a warmth of love and trust between the preacher and the people that, in the hands of God, can be used spiritually to great mutual benefit.

PART 3

RIGHTLY HANDLING
THE WORD OF TRUTH

17

Two Testaments, One Story

FOR MANY WHO TRY to understand the Bible, the process is rather like attempting to put together the pieces of a jigsaw puzzle. Certain pieces stand out and are easy to spot—identifiable by their bright colors and distinctive images. Others are obscure; where they fit into the whole is much more difficult to interpret. The Bible is a collection of sixty-six books, written over many centuries. Can they actually fit together into a coherent whole? If so, how?

In this chapter and the next, my purpose is to help you develop skills and confidence in understanding the Bible's metanarrative, its overarching storyline, which runs like a golden thread throughout its pages. Because each of the biblical authors was divinely inspired by the one divine mind, we should expect to find a consistency of content and corresponding unity of purpose through the whole biblical revelation from beginning to end. There are two testaments, but they form one united story. As my theological tutor Alec Motyer used to say, there is only one uninspired page in your Bible, which is the one the translators have inserted between the Old and New Testaments, so tear it out! Far from the Old Testament being for the Jews and the New Testament for Christians, the whole Bible is for the whole people of God and, indeed, for the whole world in every place and at every time.

The unifying principle is found in our Lord Jesus Christ himself. After his resurrection he taught his disciples, "Everything written about me in the Law of Moses and the Prophets and the Psalms must be fulfilled" (Luke 24:44). This does not mean that there is some reference to Christ in every verse of the Old Testament but that he is the key to understanding the Bible's central message—God's great plan of salvation foretold in the Old and fulfilled in the New. "Thus it is written, that the Christ should suffer and on the third day rise from the dead, and that repentance for the forgiveness of sins should be proclaimed in his name to all nations, beginning from Jerusalem" (Luke 24:46–47). When we speak about Christ in all the Scriptures, we mean that his person and work are the very center and substance of God's purposes in time and for eternity. By using this as our key interpretative principle, we are able to see how every part of Scripture contributes to the grand metanarrative and magnifies the glories of our Savior.

In the rest of the chapter, we will explore four principles to help us come to a proper understanding of Scripture as Christ centered.

1. Understanding Backward

The most obvious way to provide a framework to unify the biblical jigsaw puzzle is to read it chronologically. The story begins with creation in Genesis 1 and concludes with the new creation at the end of Revelation. The thirty-nine books of the Old Testament were written from the time of Moses (thirteenth century BC) to the prophecy of Malachi (fifth century BC). However, the story is not only told chronologically but also through the building blocks that make up the structure of the Old Testament.

The order of the Old Testament books in our English Bible reflects the Greek translation from the second century BC known as the Septuagint. Given this order, we broadly categorize the books like so: from Genesis to Esther is narrative history, from Job to Song of Solomon is wisdom, and from Isaiah to Malachi is prophecy. But the Hebrew division is rather different and is reflected in Jesus's words from

Luke 24:44. The *Law* is shorthand for the first five books of Moses, the Pentateuch, also known as the Torah (Hebrew for "instruction"). This is the foundation on which the rest of the Bible is built. The *Prophets* were divided into two. The Former Prophets (Joshua–2 Kings) are what we know as narrative history books. Since the prophet was God's mouthpiece, the inspired history recording what happened from God's perspective serves a prophetic function. God's living and enduring word takes us from the conquest of Canaan to the Babylonian exile. The Latter Prophets are those we are more familiar with—three Major Prophets (Isaiah, Jeremiah, and Ezekiel) and the twelve Minor Prophets (Hosea–Malachi). The remainder of the Old Testament is called the *Writings*. Psalms—the first and longest book of the Writings—often gave its name to the whole division.

With the coming of Christ, the centuries-long era of prediction and promise came to a close and the era of fulfillment began. That is why we rightly divide the calendar of world history by this climactic event. Everything is transformed by his life, death, resurrection, and ascension, since in this supreme intervention God's eternal purposes are finally revealed and fully realized in their sharpest focus. This means that while we must read the Bible forwards (chronologically), we can only understand it backwards (theologically). The person and work of our Lord Jesus Christ becomes the lens through which we are compelled to read and interpret the Old Testament. The old rhyme says, "The New is in the Old contained; the Old is by the New explained." And both can only be properly interpreted when Christ is the key.

Let's look at some examples of how this principle of "understanding backwards" works out in practice.

Genesis 17:7–8 and Galatians 3:7–8

In Genesis, God promises Abraham that he will establish his covenant with him and his offspring and that he will give them the land of Canaan. The emphasis is on the "everlasting" (Gen. 17:7) nature of the promise, which might lead us to see its fulfillment in the restoration of the state of Israel and their possession of the land today. But Galatians shows that the "sons of Abraham" are believers, both Jews and Gentiles, who have faith in God's promise in the gospel (Gal. 3:7). This is now fulfilled in Christ ("the offspring," Gal. 3:16) and entered into by all who are united to him by faith (see also Gal. 3:28–29).

Isaiah 11:10 and Romans 15:12

The "root of Jesse" produced the Davidic monarchy, which in Isaiah 11:10 is seen as the rallying banner for all the nations to gather under. There they will find wisdom and rest. Does this offer a future earthly, Jewish king a world-wide rule? Clearly not, according to Paul in Romans 15:12. This is no mere human ruler but Christ the King, who is the source of God's mercy to the Gentiles (see Rom. 15:8–9). The verse from Isaiah is the climax of the series of Old Testament quotations in Romans 15 in which the Gentiles rejoice in the peace and hope of the gospel through Jesus Christ.

Isaiah 28:16 and Romans 9:30–33

Isaiah rebukes the rulers of Jerusalem who trust in human allies to deliver them from the Assyrians (Isa. 28:14–15). By contrast, God is planting a foundation stone in Zion that will be sure and never disappoint those who build on it (Isa. 28:16). According to Romans 9:30–33, this is not a reference to an earthly city or temple but to Christ. Picking up Isaiah 28:16 and combining it with Isaiah 8:14, Paul shows that the stone becomes a stumbling block. He applies this to Israel's refusal of God's gift of righteousness by faith in the Messiah. Seeking to establish their righteousness on the basis of their works, they have stumbled over and rejected God's foundation stone of his new covenant community, the crucified Lord Jesus.

2. Fulfillment Not Replacement

The Old Testament belongs to the Christian church as a major encouragement to our faith, as Paul writes in Romans 15:4, "Whatever was written in former days was written for our instruction, that through endurance and through the encouragement of the Scriptures we might have hope." He also told Timothy that Scripture (the Old Testament) is profitable not only for teaching and training but also for reproof and correction (2 Tim. 3:16). So he warns the Corinthians regarding Israel's rebellion that "these things took place as examples for us, that we might not desire evil as they did" (1 Cor. 10:6). Even more powerfully, Jesus declares in the Sermon on the Mount that he has not come to abolish the Law or the Prophets but to fulfill them (Matt. 5:17). Ours is not a replacement theology but a fulfillment theology.

Sometimes, when studying an Old Testament text, Christian preachers are encouraged to ask, "Where can I find Jesus in this text?" That is a good instinct, but I don't think it is the most helpful question. It could so easily morph into "What understanding of Jesus can I force into this text?" A better question would be "What difference does it make to this text that Jesus has come?" When we have understood what it meant for its original audience, we need then to ask how the light flowing from Christ's revelation in the New Testament deepens and enriches our understanding. How does it point us to fulfillment in Christ? The later revelation is always the key to understanding the earlier revelation because of the principle of progressive or cumulative revelation, which lies at the heart of the Bible's own development of its metanarrative.

Consider the instruction that Jesus himself gives us about his relationship to the earlier revelation. "Do not think that I have come to abolish the Law or the Prophets; I have not come to abolish them but to fulfill them. For truly, I say to you, until heaven and earth pass away, not an iota, not a dot, will pass from the Law until all is accomplished" (Matt. 5:17–18). Jesus clearly states that he is the climax, focus, and fulfillment of all the Law and Prophets. Not the smallest letter or punctuation mark of the Old Testament Scriptures will be redundant or disappear until the new creation is "accomplished." Rather than their fulfilment involving the removal of old covenant teaching, Christ deepens their significance to a personal practical godliness, which exceeds the externalism of the Jewish religious leaders. For "unless your righteousness exceeds that of the scribes and Pharisees, you will never enter the kingdom of heaven" (Matt. 5:20). The examples that follow (Matt. 5:21–48) all have this point to make. Jesus takes the principle of a particular law, which expresses the unchanging eternal character of God and applies it more deeply to the internal attitudes of mind and heart. This deeper, progressive righteousness is the mark of living under Christ's kingly rule. It has been described as the manifesto of his kingdom. It is not the way into the kingdom, but it is evidence of its citizenship.

3. Continuity and Discontinuity

One of the most important ingredients of expository preaching is the bridge the preacher must construct over which the unchanging truth of the Bible text crosses—from the "them then" original context to the "us now" of our contemporary hearers. There are several important elements to keep in mind as we consider this bridge building. First, we know that the Bible is God's self-revelation. It is God's book about himself before it becomes his book about us. In Scripture we hear God preaching himself to us. That focus of divine revelation is unchanging, on both sides of the bridge. Remember that this revelation comes from God, the holy Trinity, because although the three persons are only fully revealed in the New Testament, it is eternally true that the divine being is one God. Across the centuries to our own time, there is a firm *unbroken line* from God then to God now. Nothing is different because God has not changed and never will. He is eternally the same.

The second element of bridge building between the testaments requires that we remember that much of the Old Testament records the dealings of this immutable God with his chosen people Israel. Their interaction not only teaches us the nature and character of God but also the characteristics of human nature. So can we make a connection from Israel then to the nation state of Israel today—or to humanity in general, perhaps? The answer is *no* because Christ has come. The connection we make today is to the community of covenant people who, like Old Testament Israel, have been brought into relationship with God by his grace. The line of connection runs to the church, the new covenant people of God, but it must be a *dotted line* because there are both similarities and differences, continuity and discontinuity.

The principles of entry into the old covenant and new covenant are the same—both are dependent on God's sovereign grace. But now grace extends through the gospel to all who are "sons of Abraham" by faith in Christ not by ethnic descent (Gal. 3:7–9). There is a difference not only of covenant membership (now including Jews and Gentiles) but also in terms of the covenant's operation because of the atoning death of the Lord Jesus on the cross. The sacrificial system is gone; the priesthood is redundant; the temple has been fulfilled by Christ himself as the meeting place between God and man. The festivals, food laws, rituals, and shadows of the law are fulfilled in Christ. Their work is done, and we are never to return to them because there is nothing to return to. "These are a shadow of the things to come, but the substance belongs to Christ" (Col. 2:17).

There is a third element to consider in our bridge building. We might call this element "the individual." The corporate relationship between God and Israel frequently narrows to individual members of the covenant community to whom God reveals himself and through whom he develops his purposes. Given the many characters that fill the pages of Scripture, we may be tempted to connect "them then" directly to "me now." But that is not the case. Ultimately, the gulf between the two contexts is bridged by the person and work of Christ. Of course, we can learn a great deal from God's relationship to various Old Testament characters, but we are not in their shoes and do not have to look for inspired similarity between them and us. Such comparisons would be speculative, often the product of a creative imagination rather than careful textual study. We must beware of imposing our thoughts and ideas onto biblical characters in their different contexts. For us, the line of connection travels from God through Christ so that everything we learn about God through the Old Testament revelation is now interpreted to us through Christ's own teaching and that of his divinely inspired apostles.

"Him we proclaim, warning everyone and teaching everyone with all wisdom, that we may present everyone mature in Christ" (Col. 1:28). Christ is the heart of the Bible's message, the key to its interpretation, and the glorious content of our exposition—whatever part of God's word we preach. Let's look at some specific examples to see the out-working of the principle in the ministry of Jesus.

Matthew 5:38–39

"An eye for an eye and a tooth for a tooth" (Matt. 5:38) is a direct quotation from the law in Exodus 21:24. Its purpose was to restrict vengeance by establishing the principle of an equivalence of punishment to the crime committed (i.e., not two eyes for one). There is a continuing principle of justice that the law supports and that should be administered dispassionately. But its application to Christ's disciples alerts us to a discontinuity as Jesus turns the spotlight on to the victim's reaction. Far from seeking revenge or even justice, his followers are to be willing to suffer at the hands of those who oppose them (see also Rom. 12:19). In the verses that follow (Matt. 5:39–42), Jesus gives practical examples of what that could look like in the cultural setting of his own day, but they are not difficult to translate to equivalent details in our own contemporary situation.

Mark 7:18–20

Mark 7:18–20 is set in the context of a controversy over the ritual washing of hands. Jesus uses this as an example of how the religious leaders substituted an external cleansing for inner purity (see Mark 7:1–7). He accuses them of esteeming their traditions more than God's instruction, such as the commandment to honor one's parents (Mark 7:8–13). Jesus then turns to the food laws, insisting that proscribed foods did not defile a person. The food laws were intended to be a sign of the distinctive holiness of God's people in obedience to his instruction. But Jesus teaches that this is not a matter of merely external behavior. The continuity of God's requirement of holiness is preserved, but the discontinuity is that its fulfillment is now related explicitly to the inner life of each person, not outward conformity. Christ's purpose is to perform heart surgery (see Mark 7:21–23). The initial Old Testament call to law obedience is deepened by Christ to a much more radical solution.

John 2:18–22

The Old Testament says much about the tabernacle and later the Jerusalem temple as the dwelling place of God among his people (see Ex. 25:8). In Jesus's day the temple was an impressive structure that had taken many years to build (John 2:20) but was no longer faithfully serving its purpose (John 2:16). The need for a meeting place between God and man continues to exist, but the discontinuity concerns its nature and location. Christ had come to fulfill the meeting place between God and man, not through an earthly building, but in his own body, the Word made flesh. This would be accomplished by his death and resurrection (John 2:19). As this truth is developed elsewhere in the New Testament, we are taught why earthly temples are irrelevant (John 4:21–24) and why there will be no temple in the new Jerusalem (Rev. 21:22).

4. Harmony in Diversity

The integrating principle of Christ as the center of all the Scriptures ensures that none of the Bible's contents are self-contradictory and that any interpretation that pits one part of revelation against another is bound to be erroneous. Since the purpose of Scripture is to reveal God, it is not surprising that the Old Testament law is an expression of his divine nature and character. But how does the detailed Old

Testament law code apply to us today, if we are not under the law but under God's grace (see Rom. 6:14)? Since all Scripture is given by God and profitable, how do the details of the law relate to us today when we live in such a different cultural environment? The answer is to look beneath the surface of the cultural details to the unchanging aspects of God's character that are revealed so that we can translate their purpose, through Christ, to our own context. Amid the diversity in Scripture, we discover the unchanging divine harmony. Once again, let's put flesh on the skeleton with some examples.

Deuteronomy 22:1

Deuteronomy 22:1 commands, "You shall not see your brother's ox or his sheep going astray and ignore them. You shall take them back to your brother." While it is possible that this could have a literal application today, such circumstances are outside of the everyday life experiences for most. Clearly, the principle is to love one's neighbor, which is a reflection of the compassionate love of God and which flows from our desire to please him. An ox or sheep was a valuable asset. To fail to return it to its owner expressed not merely carelessness but a total lack of concern. The principle is upheld by every action of God toward us in compassion and mercy. Thus, membership in his kingdom involves submission to his will as defined in the Golden Rule of Matthew 7:12: "So whatever you wish that others would do to you, do also to them, for this is the Law and the Prophets." The principle of neighbor love is seen supremely in the self-sacrificing love of Christ, who has met our greatest need in his atoning death on the cross. This motivates us to follow in his footsteps in showing practical compassion and care whenever we encounter others in need.

Deuteronomy 22:12

"You shall make yourself tassels on the four corners of the garment with which you cover yourself" (Deut. 22:12). The tassels were a distinctive work of Israelite clothing (Num. 15:38–39). They were an external sign of their separation from all other peoples as the covenant people of God, a mark of their privileged relationship. They were also to be a perpetual reminder to them of the moral and spiritual obligations they had toward the Lord who had brought them to himself and constituted them as a great nation. Privilege without responsibility, however, feeds pride. Thus, as with many such distinctions, by the time of the Pharisees, they seem to have been corrupted into marks of arrogance and self-promotion. The symbols had become substitutes for the reality. "They do all their deeds to be seen by others," Jesus said of them (Matt. 23:5). In contrast, Christ was willing to consecrate himself to his Father, to do his will and seek only his approval, as he offered himself on the cross as the suffering sacrifice for human sin. "Much more have the grace of God and the free gift by the grace of that one man Jesus Christ abounded for many" (Rom. 5:15). That grace is to produce in Christian believers a likeness to the Lord Jesus in terms of personal holiness as the distinguishing feature of our lives. We are not to be half-hearted or compromised in our commitment to him but to remind ourselves every day whose we are and whom we serve. Dig beneath the cultural diversity to the harmony of the unchanging principle, grounded in God himself.

18

The Skeleton Structure

TO DEVELOP AS COMPETENT PREACHERS, we have to learn to carefully select the words we use to achieve maximum clarity and impact. But we also have to think carefully about the structure of our sermons: How do the ideas flow from one to another? Where are the major emphases? How much time do we intend to take on each point? Preaching is a serious responsibility because in Scripture we have a God-given message with life-changing potential, so we want to harness all our skills and abilities to reach the minds, hearts, and wills of our hearers.

Although they are inspired by the Holy Spirit, Bible writers operate in exactly the same way. In his sovereignty, God has used a variety of communication approaches to convey his eternal truth. Much of the Bible began its life as the spoken word, and all of it is intended to be read aloud, so we need to pay careful attention to the structure of each unit and to the type of speech or writing being employed.

The Skeleton Structure in Genesis 1–11

It has been said that the Bible is a book of two halves—Genesis 1–11 and the rest! Certainly, the first eleven chapters of the Bible provide us with the seedbed from which all the later growth springs. But they also provide us with a structure for the big picture story of all the sixty-six books. The coherence of the whole unit is conveyed through its chronology. From the account of creation, we move to the fall and its repercussions, then on to the flood and the Noah rescue story, and ultimately to the scattering of the peoples resulting from the Tower of Babel. The genre is narrative, and the sequence is historical, but built into this structure is the theological significance of these events. Because this is God's revelation, the story is told from his standpoint. We see that from the beginning God is the prime mover and the central figure in the unfolding narrative.

The book of Genesis is divided into sections by its own internal marker, translated as "This is the generation of." The Hebrew formula, coming from the verb "to beget" or "to give life to," might equally be translated as "This is what came out of that." It teaches not only the historical sequence of what came next but also the theological cause and effect process, which gives the divine perspective on the human events. For example, it appears in Genesis 2:4 between the majestic creation overture of Genesis 1 and the more domestic and personal details of Adam and Eve in the garden in Genesis 2. This is what came out of that. But perhaps its function is most clearly seen in Genesis 6:9. The preceding verse tells us that "Noah found favor in the eyes of the LORD" (Gen. 6:8). A pattern is being established that will run through the whole Bible. God's unmerited favor, his grace, selects Noah for rescue from the flood as a sovereign act of his saving mercy. Noah's subsequent righteousness is the outcome of the divine choice, *not* the reason for it.

When we compare the three major events of these chapters, post-creation, we see a skeleton structure emerging that will be replicated in all that follows.

Episode 1: Adam and Eve

The fall, in Genesis 3, is an act of deliberate rebellion against the instruction of God: "Of the tree of the knowledge of good and evil you shall not eat" (Gen. 2:17). It is an attack by the creature upon the authority of the Creator. It is a refusal to let God be God, motivated by the desire to be like God (Gen. 3:5). This is the essence of sin. Inevitably this rebellion calls out God's righteous judgment in retribution. The serpent is cursed, and the rebellious couple is evicted from the garden, destined now for a life marked by pain and toil. Sin leads to judgment, alienation, and punishment. But at the same time there is a divine intervention of mercy. The shame of Adam and Eve is covered by garments made for them by God (Gen. 3:21). More importantly, God promises that the woman's offspring will crush the serpent's head (Gen. 3:15). Here is a glimmer of hope, a prospect of change, perhaps even of salvation. The pattern is clear: sin leads to retribution, but divine intervention in mercy promises deliverance through rescue.

Episode 2: Noah

The Noah story reveals the same characteristics but on a much larger canvas. The rebellion is universal (Gen. 6:12–13), and the retribution must be equivalent. But even with the announcement of impending destruction in the flood, God instructs Noah to build an ark. Thus, provision is made for the great rescue of his family and the representative animals. Noah experiences the judgment, but secure in the ark (God's provision) he is saved and carried into the new world that lies beyond. And that new world is marked by God's restored relationship with his creation, sealed by covenant promise and a covenant sign in the form of the rainbow (Gen. 9:9–13). The pattern of rescue emerges through a divinely provided deliverance, motivated entirely by God's grace and mercy.

Noah was saved out of a world under God's righteous judgment by God's sovereign choice. God chose the man and the means. Noah initiated nothing; he simply obeyed in faith (Heb. 11:7). Yet in this interaction we find all the basic ingredients of the covenant, which will become the context in which God will always deal with those whom he chooses. It is not a bargain struck between equals, like a contract.

How could it be? Rather, the covenant is a unilateral pledge, by God, to provide a means of salvation from his righteous judgment, resting on his free choice but operating with justice.

Since this is the skeleton structure for the whole biblical story, the apostles have no difficulty applying it to the experience of salvation for sinful people of every nation through the sacrifice of our Lord Jesus Christ. Peter, reminding his readers that "Christ also suffered once for sins, the righteous for the unrighteous, that he might bring us to God" (1 Pet. 3:18), relates this to the parallel in the story of Noah:

> God's patience waited in the days of Noah, while the ark was being prepared, in which a few, that is, eight persons, were brought safely through water. Baptism, which corresponds to this, now saves you, not as a removal of dirt from the body but as an appeal to God for a good conscience, through the resurrection of Jesus Christ. (1 Pet. 3:20–21)

In baptism, the Christian believer is momentarily submerged under the hostile medium of the water, a symbol of death (judgment) and of identification with Christ who suffered death as punishment for the sins of his people. Just as the water that brought judgment was for Noah the means by which he was transferred into a new life, so the Christian believer, dying with Christ, is raised with him to newness of life. The pledge of salvation is fulfilled solely through God's grace, but his deliverance operates with justice because the price of sin has been paid.

Episode 3: The Tower of Babel

In episode 3 of Genesis 1–11, the account of the Tower of Babel demonstrates the unmistakably clear pattern of human rebellion that prompts God's righteous retribution. "Come, let us build ourselves a city and a tower with its top in the heavens, and let us make a name for ourselves, lest we be dispersed over the face of the whole earth" (Gen. 11:4). The story repeats: the attempt to dethrone God and to exalt the human self in his place. The irony is that the scattering they feared is precisely the outcome of their arrogant rebellion. The Lord came down and "confused the language of all the earth" (Gen. 11:9). Sin leads to retribution. But where is God's grace? Where is the hope of salvation in this third great act of judgment? The next verse provides the answer: "These are the generations of Shem"—that is, Noah's eldest son (Gen. 11:10). And by Genesis 11:26, we have reached Terah and his son Abram. As with Noah, so after Babel, God begins again with a new representative man with whom he will enter into covenant. For the next thirteen chapters, Abraham is the chief human figure in the story.

More Flesh on the Skeleton

While Genesis 1–11 is certainly a historical account of the earliest times, it is not *merely* that. Rather, it is the seedbed that provides the pattern or skeleton for the metanarrative of the whole Bible. The Creator God desires to restore relationship and peace with human kind. He does this through his own saving grace, meeting the claims of his justice and opening the way to a covenant—a divinely-created fellowship with reconciled sinners. What begins as the experience of a single individual is destined eventually to become universal in scope. And at the heart of the covenant lies the principle of substitutionary sacrifice, which opens the door to restored fellowship and requires the response of faith and obedience.

It is particularly instructive to trace the pattern as it emerges through all the key moments of Old Testament history. Abraham learns that God himself will provide the sacrificial offering in the place of his only son, Isaac (Gen. 22). As his family develops and multiplies into the great nation of Israel, they too learn the principle that the only safe shelter from the righteous judgment of a holy God is to be found in the blood of the Passover lamb—a remedy for each individual family and so for the whole nation (Ex. 12). All the ups and downs of Israel's ensuing history underscore the pattern in many different contexts, but

God is always active to produce a people faithful to him, reflecting his faithfulness to them. So often throughout the biblical storyline, sin and rebellion seem to be in control, and many acts of divine judgment are the inevitable consequences. But every time, God's mercy reaches out to provide a way of escape or rescue, which has to be embraced by faith and obedience.

For example, consider the snakes in the wilderness in Numbers 21:4–9. The Israelites are impatient and ungrateful, despising God's gracious provision of the daily manna (Num. 21:4–5). This sin is visited by the retributive judgment of a plague of snakes, resulting in many deaths (Num. 21:6). But in response to the people's confession and Moses's prayer, God commands the making of a bronze serpent set on a pole so that whoever looks to it will live (Num. 21:7–8). Merciful divine intervention leads to deliverance. Moses obeys God's instruction, and those who exercise faith by doing what God commands live (Num. 21:9). Here is more flesh on the skeleton: sin leads to retribution, but divine intervention in grace and mercy provides deliverance. It is no wonder that the Lord Jesus himself uses this event to explain to Nicodemus how he will be lifted up to die and bring eternal life to all who believe in him (John 3:14–15)— fulfilling the prophetic imagery.

The skeleton structure supplies the theme tune for the book of Judges. Judges 2:11–23 provides a summary of the narratives that follow. Israel abandons God their rescuer through the sin of idolatry, serving the gods of the pagan nations around them (Judg. 2:11–13). They provoked the Lord to anger as they trampled his covenant under their feet, so he gave them over to invaders who plundered them and triumphed over them (Judg. 2:14–15). "And they were in terrible distress" (Judg. 2:15), but God intervened to raise up judges as saviors to rescue them from their enemies (2:16). This happened because "the LORD was moved to pity by their groaning," and so he was with the judge to save them (Judg. 2:18). Their oppression was lifted, but only during the lifetime of the rescuing judge. Sadly, the pattern was repeated so often by renewed sin and rebellion that eventually God's power to deliver was withdrawn (Judg. 2:19–23).

Yet through all the centuries of Old Testament history, the promise of the serpent-crushing deliverer shines with increasing clarity and brilliance. Think, for example, of the wonderful servant songs of Isaiah (Isa. 42:1–4; 49:1–6; 50:4–11; 52:13–53:12). Even the greatest of the patriarchs, kings, or prophets could not fulfill that role. Until one day on the banks of the river Jordan, the last great prophet cried out, "Behold, the Lamb of God, who takes away the sin of the world!" (John 1:29)—a perfect human sacrifice for human sin, for everyone everywhere.

Perhaps the full flesh on the skeleton is presented most powerfully to us in Romans 5:1–11, one of the greatest expositions of the gospel. The passage describes the human condition with devastating honesty. We are "weak" (unable to help ourselves) and "ungodly" (Rom. 5:6) "sinners" (5:8). The consequences of our sin are both implicit—our natural hostility toward God (Rom. 5:1)—and explicit—God's righteous wrath toward us (5:9). We are enemies, alienated and cut off from God (Rom. 5:10–11). However, the heart of the passage is the wonderful divine intervention that meets our abject need: "Christ died for the ungodly" (Rom. 5:6), "Christ died for us" (5:8). Through his blood we are saved from wrath, reconciled to God by Christ's death, and saved by his resurrection life (Rom. 5:9–10). Throughout the passage, this salvation and deliverance is celebrated. We have peace, access to God, joy, and hope—even in suffering (Rom. 5:1–4). "God's love has been poured into our hearts through the Holy Spirit" (Rom. 5:5), and through that mercy we are justified (5:1, 9) and reconciled (5:10–11).

Four Questions for Seeing the Skelton Structure

Through the skeleton structure, we are helped to see why Christ is the center of all the Scriptures and why the story of God's loving purposes in human history revolves around and finds its focus in him. Whatever passage of the Bible we may be dealing with, the pattern of the metanarrative, this skeleton structure, is always a key tool to use. To do this, answer the following four questions about the text you are studying:

1. How does the passage relate to God, the Creator and Redeemer? (This is a more focused way of asking what God is teaching about himself in the passage.)
2. What do we learn about his sovereign grace?
3. How does the passage point us forward to the ultimate solution in the person and work of our Lord Jesus Christ?
4. What response does this require from us in terms of covenant faith and obedience?

The rich variety of biblical literature is ultimately designed to produce this outcome: that we are "looking to Jesus, the founder and perfecter of our faith" (Heb. 12:2). Using the four questions above, let us look at three representative examples of how the tool can help us in our preaching.

2 Samuel 9:1–13

This is the narrative in which King David showed "the kindness of God" (2 Sam. 9:3) to Mephibosheth, the crippled son of Jonathan.

Question 1: David's action reveals the nature of God. Two chapters earlier, David himself experienced God's kindness through his promises to David and his dynasty. Speaking of David's son, God says, "My steadfast love will not depart from him. . . . And your house and your kingdom shall be made sure forever before me" (2 Sam. 7:15–16). David prefigures his greatest Son, the Messiah.

Question 2: There is not the slightest compulsion on David to be gracious. In fact, we might have expected him to eliminate all of Saul's descendants. Perhaps this is what Mephibosheth expected when he fell on his face and paid homage to David, describing himself as a "dead dog" (2 Sam. 9:8). David's grace is offered in his kingly sovereignty, and it is entirely unexpected.

Question 3: Great David's greater Son shows his undeserved favor to those who are dead in sin. Mephibosheth was crippled and entirely dependent on the kindness of others, as are all sinners before God. The steadfast love and kindness of the Lord Jesus on the cross provides us a place at the table of his heavenly banquet, just as Mephibosheth always ate at the king's table (2 Sam. 9:10).

Question 4: Our response is to receive our King's offer (see Ps. 23:5) in awe and wonder at the grace of God in the gospel. We experience joy in receiving all the undeserved blessings that are ours in Christ, and we seek to live in obedience to our Lord because of his kindness (see Titus 3:4–5).

1 Kings 17:8–16

The narrative describes how a widow of Zarephath sustains Elijah in a time of famine and is herself miraculously sustained by God's provision.

Question 1: Elijah pronounced God's judgment on Israel in the form of a prolonged drought. They had turned away from the Creator God who provides rain and harvests. Instead, they worshiped the Baals, the false nature gods of Queen Jezebel. But because God is sovereign over the whole of his creation he is able to sustain his servant by the most unlikely of means—ravens (1 Kings 17:6) and a foreign widow (17:9).

Question 2: God's gracious provision operates in the most hostile circumstances. It reaches out to the widow and her son, who are outside the covenant people but she is prepared to act on what God says to her through his prophet. When the human agents take their place under divine sovereignty, God miraculously provides.

Question 3: Although the woman believes she and her son will die (1 Kings 17:12), Elijah is the human means by which God saves them. She has nothing, but she acts in faith on God's word, providing the prophet with a little cake. Then she experiences the replenishment of her flour and oil by the Lord "for many days" (1 Kings 17:15). The parallel with Christ's work is seen in his unending supernatural provision of spiritual life and sustenance to those who trust and obey him.

Question 4: The widow experienced God's offered blessing through faith, which expressed itself in obedience to his word (1 Kings 17:15). The promise of God was, as always, completely reliable and fulfilled. But this was only proved to her when faith overcame her fear (1 Kings 17:13). The pagan widow did what the nation of Israel had failed to do.

Luke 7:11–17

This brief narrative recounts the miracle of Jesus raising the only son of the widow of Nain.

Question 1: Throughout his ministry, the Lord Jesus revealed the glory of the unseen Father as the Word made flesh full of grace and truth. In this passage, the emphasis is on the divine "compassion" (Luke 7:13) for the bereaved mother. She is a widow, engulfed in grief for her only son. Her divine rescuer knows what it is to bear our griefs and carry our sorrows (Isa. 53:4).

Question 2: Jesus demonstrates his sovereignty as the author and giver of life. In this he is utterly unique. No one else could raise the dead to life by his powerful word. His mercy is directed toward both the widow and her son, but he also causes the crowd to glorify God (Luke 7:15–16).

Question 3: Although the young man is raised, he will inevitably die again. Only Christ can conquer the enemy of death by a permanent triumph in his own death and resurrection. The death of Jesus finished the work so that in his risen power he brings eternal life to all who believe in him (John 11:25–26).

Question 4: The truth of the story compels us to face the question of the identity of Jesus. Who is this man who raises the dead? It also underlines the life-giving power of his word, one of the great themes of Luke's Gospel. For those who believe, it is a great encouragement to keep trusting his compassion and grace—even through tears—and to focus on the eternal life that is ours through his work.

19

Keep On Keeping On

ONE OF THE MOST IMPORTANT QUALITIES for the expository preacher to cultivate is perseverance, the ability to persist with the task through thick and thin. If producing an expository sermon takes several hours, producing the preacher takes a lifetime. This is because both the skills and godliness of character required are strongly interconnected and take time to develop to maturity. This is God's way in God's world, and preaching is no exception to the rule. We never stop learning, and we are constantly challenged to improve.

At first that may sound daunting, even discouraging, but actually it is the opposite. In our culture of instant gratification, we want to be able to do everything quickly and with minimal effort, but none of life's really worthwhile ingredients can be achieved that way. Whatever sphere of activity we operate in, excellence requires hard work, dedication, discipline, and more hard work. But the motivation to keep pressing on lies in the supreme value and significance of what we are doing and in the fact that we can, and do, make steady progress. For most of us, that will be the pattern of our preaching ministry. Every time we proclaim God's truth, the possibilities are unlimited and the potential consequences are eternal, which is why biblical preaching matters so much.

In every generation there are some outstanding preachers who are unusually gifted by God. We benefit from them, admire them, and thank God for them. We may even try to copy them, but that never works. Each of us is a unique individual, shaped and gifted by the same Lord for the specific tasks of ministry he has for us to fulfill. We are not called to replicate someone else but to be ourselves, in Christ. By dependence on his Spirit, we are to grow in both competence and character, day by day, week by week. As we have the privilege of time set aside to study God's word in depth, it must first do its work in our own hearts and lives, producing the fruit of Christ-like character. Before we can ever teach or admonish others, the sword of God's Spirit must do its work on us, at the center of our beings, teaching, reproving, correcting, and training us. Only then can God's servant become competent, "equipped for every good work" (2 Tim. 3:17). But as we make progress, we shall become increasingly aware of our own incompetence, not only in our preaching skills but especially in the deficiencies of character—still so unlike the Lord Jesus. But this is what the life of faith, through grace, is all about. What God is looking for is progress (1 Tim. 4:15–16).

There will always be a holy discontent in the heart of the Bible preacher: I should be doing the job much better. I should be godlier than I am. I pray to be able to present myself to God "as one approved, a worker who has no need to be ashamed, rightly handling the word of truth" (2 Tim. 2:15). I long and labor to be "a vessel for honorable use, set apart as holy, useful to the master of the house, ready for every good work" (2 Tim. 2:21). But the fact that we have not already obtained this, that we are not already the finished article, is not a disincentive but a spur to keep pressing on. Thank God for all the progress he has enabled you to make, but don't give up on perseverance and persistence. Trust him for the hard work ahead. Invest in whatever will strengthen and improve your preaching. Above all, ensure that exposition of the word is the heartbeat, the engine room, of all your ministry.

Paul, the Trailblazer

Paul's second letter to Timothy has long been recognized as one of the most illuminating, challenging, and empowering Bible texts to inform and inspire the pastor-teacher. Written to address Timothy's challenging situation in Ephesus, the letter's exhortations and imperatives are as immediately relevant to God's servants today as they were then. "Do not be ashamed of the testimony about our Lord, . . . but share in suffering for the gospel by the power of God" (2 Tim. 1:8). "Follow the pattern of the sound words" (2 Tim. 1:13). "Be strengthened by the grace that is in Christ Jesus" (2 Tim. 2:1). As always in Scripture, the instruction and exhortation are totally interwoven. That becomes even clearer as the letter proceeds, with its confidence that "all Scripture is breathed out by God" (2 Tim. 3:16), leading to the great charge in the light of the eternal kingdom to "preach the word" (4:2).

However, the end of the letter is where Paul reviews and reflects on his ministry in light of his imminent departure, which helps us identify and reaffirm our own ministry priorities as we dedicate ourselves to the long haul. In 2 Timothy 4:7–8, Paul writes, "I have fought the good fight, I have finished the race, I have kept the faith. Henceforth there is laid up for me the crown of righteousness, which the Lord, the righteous judge, will award to me on that day, and not only to me but also to all who have loved his appearing." It is one thing to start well in ministry, but it is another to end well. Yet here is the great apostle ending well and providing us with invaluable insights into his own perspective and priorities of ministry. If we are to follow in his footsteps, we shall need to be cultivating these convictions and qualities in our own service.

"I Have Fought the Good Fight"

Paul sees his ministry as a struggle that required great dedication and exertion. But it was a good fight, well worth all the effort, since it concerned righteousness and gospel truth triumphing over the evil of a rebellious and godless world. Paul has described the difficulties of the last days, when "people will be lovers of self, lovers of money . . . lovers of pleasure rather than lovers of God" (2 Tim. 3:2, 4). And these distorted values were even beginning to penetrate and poison the Ephesian church, where some were "having the appearance of godliness, but denying its power" (2 Tim. 3:5; see 3:6–7). Fighting with the word of God against the world, the flesh, and the devil is the calling and solemn responsibility of every biblical preacher. But soldiers can and do become wounded. The ministry Paul entrusted to Timothy to pass on God's revealed truth to "faithful men, who will be able to teach others also" (2 Tim. 2:2) was always going to provoke opposition and personal attack. This is why he exhorted Timothy, "Share in suffering as a good soldier of Christ Jesus. No soldier gets entangled in civilian pursuits, since his aim is to please the one who enlisted him" (2 Tim. 2:3–4).

The danger is that we will be distracted by "civilian pursuits" and so become divided in our loyalties. We should not take this to mean the proper duties of family life or our responsible involvement in our community, of course, but we must not allow these to distract us from fighting the good fight with the word of truth. This is especially the case when we meet opposition and hostility, not only in the world but in the church. It is easy to give in to the temptation to dilute biblical truth, or to soft-pedal its demands in order to spare ourselves the pain of suffering. However, as soon as we start to do that, the Bible is no longer in the driver's seat. In fact, our opponents have taken control and a battle has been lost. Sadly, one compromise leads to another until another soldier is effectively neutralized and the cause of Christ suffers another setback. What will keep us faithful is making it our aim to please the one who enlisted us and recognizing that, while we serve in time, it is within the context of eternity.

"I Have Finished the Race"

Paul testifies that he has completed the course allotted to him (2 Tim. 4:7). He has kept on track and adhered to the rules of the competition.

In 2 Timothy 2:5 he follows the soldier metaphor with that of the athlete, reminding Timothy, "An athlete is not crowned unless he competes according to the rules." The crown at the end of the course is in view for the apostle, and he is confident that nothing will disqualify him. The work has been done and the mission accomplished. As Jesus affirmed to his Father at the end of his earthly race, "I glorified you on earth, having accomplished the work that you gave me to do" (John 17:4).

If we are to be able to humbly say the same at the end of our course, we shall have to keep on track, doing God's work in God's way, dependent on both word and Spirit in study, prayer, and proclamation. That means we will not accomplish many things well-meaning people have lined up for us to do. Our determined choice must be to run the race our master sets before us and to do so as faithfully as we can. He is the content of our preaching ("him we proclaim," Col. 1:28), and he is the only one whose approval we seek for our service. Stick with his priorities!

"I Have Kept the Faith"

The use of "the" before "faith" (2 Tim. 4:7) implies more than just loyalty. Paul charges Timothy to "guard the good deposit" (2 Tim. 1:14)—that is, the gospel, God's revealed truth. Paul's testimony that he has kept the faith likely refers back to the third picture of faithful service in 2 Timothy 2:6: "It is the hard-working farmer who ought to have the first share of the crops." The emphasis is on dedicated work in the present in anticipation of the fruit of future blessings. Paul has faithfully preserved the precious deposit of the gospel of God's truth. The fruits of this are visible in the churches around the Mediterranean world, which will be recognized when he receives "the crown of righteousness" (2 Tim. 4:8). He has kept the faith by constantly sowing the seed of the gospel and teaching the churches how to live in order to please God. He has taught the truth, the whole truth, and nothing but the truth. There has been no deviation, no compromise. Always and everywhere, Paul has sown the good seed of the word, and like the earthly farmer he has trusted the Lord of the harvest to do his work by bringing many into his kingdom.

The crown of righteousness, or justification, is not Paul's reward for his service. Above all else he remains a sinner, justified by God's amazing grace. And so are we! The gospel was just as central to his own life as it was to his faithful ministry. He expressed this reality to Timothy earlier in the letter, reminding him that God "saved us and called us to a holy calling, not because of our works but because of his own purpose and grace, which he gave us in Christ Jesus before the ages began" (2 Tim. 1:9). He is not motivated by a reward. It will be enough for Paul to be vindicated, justified before the righteous Judge, even though a Roman court may condemn him. On the last day, the only day that ultimately matters, he will be declared righteous and accepted by the one whose assessment truly counts, and not only Paul but "all who have loved his appearing" (2 Tim. 4:8). That includes us, as we seek to serve him now in our generation, motivated by the eternal perspective of the King in all his glory for whom we long.

Perspectives to Nurture

I want to conclude by presenting a collage of biblical texts supporting four indispensable perspectives that we need to embrace and actively cultivate if we are to keep faithfully persevering and growing in our competence to preach the word.

Confidence in the Total Authority of Scripture

The whole Bible testifies to the essential need of God's self-revelation in the Scriptures if we are to know anything about God with certainty. There are many things we cannot know, but what God has revealed is given to us so that we may live in right relationship with him. "The secret things belong to the LORD our God, but the things that are revealed belong to us and to our children forever, that we may do all the words of this law" (Deut. 29:29). That relationship can be nourished and deepened only by "every word that comes from the mouth of God" (Matt. 4:4, quoting Deut. 8:3). All that God has spoken is his sufficient word for godly living.

> Every word of God proves true;
>> he is a shield to those who take refuge in him.
> Do not add to his words,
>> lest he rebuke you and you be found a liar. (Prov. 30:5–6)

Our confidence in the inspiration and total authority of Scripture is further strengthened by verses from the New Testament. "Breathed out by God," the Scriptures both make us "wise for salvation" and equip us "for every good work" to live a life pleasing to God (2 Tim. 3:15–17). The apostle Peter attributes their origin to a supernatural work of the Holy Spirit (2 Pet. 1:21), which is why they are always living and active in instructing and encouraging the people of God (Rom. 15:4).

The Spirit is not only active in inspiring the writers of the Bible but also in illuminating the understanding of its readers. As Paul taught the Corinthians, God's cross-centered wisdom and power will always appear as folly to unbelievers, however intelligent they may be, since they are "spiritually discerned" (1 Cor. 2:14). God reveals his truth "through the Spirit," who grants understanding of "the things freely given us by God" (1 Cor. 2:10, 12). This is a great incentive to keep praying for the Spirit's ministry both in our study and through our proclamation. As we see the word at work in our own lives and in those whom we serve, the conviction deepens that though heaven and earth will pass away, the word of the Lord endures forever (Isa. 40:8; Mark 13:31).

Competence in the Hard Work of Ministry

After my many years of preaching, people sometimes say to me, "I suppose it doesn't take you long to produce a sermon these days," to which I reply, "Are they really that bad?" There is a common fallacy that, with experience, preparation becomes faster, slicker, and more effortless. And preachers are tempted to succumb to that fallacy. Allocating less time for preparation, cutting corners, and relying on well-tried formulas can all become subtle substitutes for the hard work that Scripture exhorts us to put in (Col. 1:28–2:1; 2 Tim. 2:15). Many ministries lose impetus and fail to achieve their full potential because of weakness in the area of personal discipline. "Every athlete exercises self-control in all things. They do it to receive a perishable wreath, but we an imperishable. So I do not run aimlessly; I do not box as one beating the air" (1 Cor. 9:25–26).

Another challenge to our perseverance in biblical ministry is the inevitable suffering involved. In 2 Timothy 1:8–12, Paul opens a window into understanding what his ministry cost him personally. He attributes his suffering directly to his appointment as "a preacher and apostle and teacher" (2 Tim. 1:11). While he reminds Timothy that "all who desire to live a godly life in Christ Jesus will be persecuted" (2 Tim. 3:12), clearly every faithful gospel preacher will to some extent share in Christ's suffering by serving a rejected Savior. This is why our personal times of disciplined study provide such a vital ingredient of our perseverance. As we reflect on the divine dynamic of the gospel, rejoicing that Christ has "abolished death and brought life and immortality to light through the gospel" (2 Tim. 1:10), we find new motivation to follow in his footsteps. There is an eternal perspective to all our ministry now, which is for the sake of his body, the church, "so that as grace extends to more and more people it may increase thanksgiving, to the glory of God" (2 Cor. 4:15).

But the most important element in securing our developing and continuing ministry competence is that of persevering prayer. Acts 6:4 reminds us that prayer and ministry of the word were the earliest apostolic priorities, and the order is significant—prayer before preaching. Like Paul, we need to ask others to join with us in praying for competence in our ministry. "Finally, brothers, pray for us, that the word of the Lord may speed ahead and be honored, as happened among you, and that we may be delivered from wicked and evil men" (2 Thess. 3:1–2). His concern is for the growth of the word and for his own protection in order to be able to continue this work. Similarly, he exhorts the Ephesians to be

> praying at all times in the Spirit, with all prayer and supplication. To that end, keep alert with all perseverance, making supplication for all the saints, and also for me, that words may be given to me in opening my mouth boldly to proclaim the mystery of the gospel, for which I am an ambassador in chains, that I may declare it boldly, as I ought to speak. (Eph. 6:18–20)

There is never a situation in which prayer is not needed or in which God's answers to prayer cannot make the difference. According to Paul, the gospel messenger especially needs to pray (and be prayed for) concerning the content of the message ("that words may be given"), for boldness, and for faithfulness. Try to develop a group of prayer supporters to pray with you for these ingredients as you build your ministry on prayer, keeping "alert with all perseverance."

Commitment to the Bible's Eternal Focus

A further incentive to perseverance is the constant reminder that the future eternal realities should govern our present ministries. There are many Bible passages that encourage us to nurture this perspective, and it is good to revisit them regularly as spiritual "watering holes."

In Psalm 73:23–26, there is a real expectation of future glory (73:24b) generated by the writer's experience of God's presence (73:23a), protection (73:23b), guidance (73:24a), and strength (73:26). These realities prompt his assertion that God is his greatest desire in heaven or on earth (Ps. 73:25). The light from the future encourages him to keep trusting in the present. On this side of the cross and resurrection, with the future so much clearer, Paul adds his testimony to the motivation of the eternal perspective: "I press on" (Phil. 3:12), "straining forward to what lies ahead" (3:13); "I press on toward the goal for the prize of the upward call" (3:14). The perspective of eternity is a tremendous motivation to keep on keeping on in the work God has given us.

In 2 Corinthians 4:16–18, Paul's faith for the future is based on what God has already done in the past: he "raised the Lord Jesus" (4:14). This reality explains why he does not lose heart. In the midst of physical decline and affliction, the resurrection of Jesus is the proof of the unseen eternal realities (2 Cor. 4:16–18). The "eternal weight of glory beyond all comparison" (2 Cor. 4:17) is what keeps Paul pressing on, not giving up or neglecting his calling. As he wrote in 1 Corinthians 3:11–15, the day of Christ's return will reveal the quality of a minister's workmanship and the materials used in this present time of building. With enduring materials, Paul wants to build the church, shaped by its only foundation, Jesus Christ. Again, the future motivates the apostle to the highest qualities of earthly service in the present—as it should do for us too.

Above all, the Lord Jesus teaches us in Matthew 6:19–21 that it is possible to lay up for ourselves "treasures in heaven" (6:20). In view of that eternal reality, we should invest our earthly resources in what will last and be secure. The priorities we live by will demonstrate where our time and affections lie (Matt. 6:21). The Lord exhorts us to "seek first the kingdom of God and his righteousness, and all these [earthly] things will be added to you" (Matt. 6:33). God is unfailingly faithful to those who treasure his kingdom as their greatest good. We do not need to fear for our lives being sustained in this world because we have a heavenly Father who will provide. This sets us free to invest our lives for eternity.

Concern for God's Greater Glory

God's greater glory is a powerful stimulus to perseverance. A number of New Testament texts help us translate this concept into reality.

Jesus said, "Let your light shine before others, so that they may see your good works and give glory to your Father who is in heaven" (Matt. 5:16). Consistent godly living is a means for God's light to shine, which brings him glory. Therefore, we want to encourage this response in our pastoral preaching. We also want to exhort our hearers to prove Paul's words in their own experience: "We all, with unveiled face, beholding the glory of the Lord, are being transformed into the same image from one degree of glory to another" (2 Cor. 3:18). The gospel brings us to see God's glory in Jesus, which has transforming power, making us increasingly like him as the image of God is restored in his redeemed people. That is why we "proclaim . . . Jesus Christ as Lord," since he is the source of "the light of the knowledge of the glory of God," which is to shine from our "jars of clay" (2 Cor. 4:5–7). The more we and our hearers grow in Christlikeness, the more God will be glorified in our ministries.

God's glory is further enhanced by the exaltation of the Lord Jesus and the eclipse of the messenger, as John the Baptist emphasized: "He must increase, but I must decrease" (John 3:30). For Paul, this meant that what people thought of him was of no great significance. He points out that he is only a servant and a steward in whom faithfulness is the essential requirement (1 Cor. 4:1–2). Human judgment is irrelevant because heart motives are hidden from human eyes; the day of the Lord's coming will be the only valid time for assessment (1 Cor. 4:3–5). His aim is to bring glory to God by his faithfulness. An example of this is recorded in Acts 13:44–48. In turning from the unbelieving synagogue congregation in Antioch to the Gentiles, Paul quotes Isaiah:

I have made you a light for the Gentiles,
    that you may bring salvation to the ends of the earth.
    (Acts 13:47, quoting Isa. 49:6)

Luke adds that "when the Gentiles heard this, they began rejoicing and glorifying the word of the Lord, and as many as were appointed to eternal life believed" (Acts 13:48). God's glory is enhanced by faithful gospel preaching and its outcome in repentance and faith.

Finally, additional texts illustrate ways by which God's word at work in the lives of his people brings greater glory to him. These passages provide us with worthy, biblical aims to keep pursuing in our preaching ministry. In John 15:8 Jesus speaks of "much fruit" in the lives of his disciples bringing glory to the Father. The fruit is produced by the vine's life flowing through the branches, so godly character is primarily in view. Romans 15:5–7 shows that God is glorified when the church lives in "harmony with one another," declares God's truth in unity "with one voice," and "welcome[s] one another" in love. This is the gift of the "God of endurance and encouragement" to his believing people (Rom. 15:5). Generous giving to others in need as the fruit of gospel faith is another means of glorifying God (2 Cor. 9:12–13). Furthermore, Paul's prayer for the Thessalonians is "that our God may make you worthy of his calling and may fulfill every resolve for good and every work of faith by his power, so that the name of our Lord Jesus may be glorified in you, and you in him, according to the grace of our God and the Lord Jesus Christ" (2 Thess. 1:11–12). All of these are worthy aims and outcomes of a ministry that is concerned supremely for God's greater glory.

These, then, are some of the biblical indications of how to be a faithfully persevering preacher of the word. Suffering, hard work, and personal discipline are all central to this privileged calling, but the benefits far outweigh any sacrifices. Fruitfulness, fulfillment, the word at work, joy in serving, and assurance of faith are just a few of the blessings that come from faithful word ministry. No other task is more important, and no other investment will yield such eternal dividends. So we must keep on keeping on, in season and out of season, sober-minded, enduring suffering, doing the work of an evangelist, and so fulfilling our ministry (2 Tim. 4:2, 5). We have our Bibles, so let us give ourselves to the hard work of study in the word. We have our knees, so let us pray constantly. As we give ourselves to prayer and preaching, let us trust God to enable us to become workers who do not need to be ashamed, rightly handling the word of truth. By God's grace alone and through his power alone, may we become increasingly equipped to preach the word!

A Dedication Prayer

Heavenly Father, we praise you that you have caused all Scripture to be written for our learning. Increase in us the skills to handle Holy Scripture wisely and faithfully, that we may ourselves grow daily in our knowledge and love of you and, thus, be channels of your grace as we seek to preach it to others. Help us to listen to your word and digest its truth. Empower us by your Holy Spirit to respond in faith and obedience to all that you teach. Enable us by that same Spirit to preach the word in all its fullness, faithfully and boldly, to all whom you have given us as pastor-teachers. These things we ask for the blessing of your church and for the greater glory of your name, through Jesus Christ our Lord. Amen.

Appendix

Sample Assessment

THIS SAMPLE ASSESSMENT is a tool that a preacher can use for self-evaluation but is probably best used by a listening group. There is more detail in the questions than can profitably be used in a single session. Rather, it is designed to address a range of features and issues, any of which could be profitably employed in a critique. Although it would be best to cover material from all four sections eventually, one could begin by selecting questions from each section according to the given sermon and the preacher's stage of development. Pay special attention to the explanations beneath the questions, which will help to develop the use of the assessment in a positive and creative way.

Section 1: Aim and Structure

1. *Was there a clear structure to the sermon? If so, what were the main points?*
   This is not designed to impose a particular homiletical pattern or method on the text but to ask whether the Bible text was in the driver's seat and whether the structure of the talk reflected the structure of the original passage with accuracy and clarity.

2. *Was there a clear message? What was it?*
   The message should represent the content of the passage but be presented in more than a merely informational way. A message is something deeper

and more urgent. It is communication through the mind, to the heart, to activate the will. So if preaching is designed to change lives—to make us more like the Lord Jesus—in what way did the sermon accomplish that?

3. *Was the introduction engaging and appropriate? Did the sermon deliver what the introduction promised?*

The introduction should provide a menu for the sermon and draw the hearer in. It may pose a question or draw an application that the rest of the talk will answer or expand. Consider whether it was integral to what followed or disconnected.

4. *Was there a clear conclusion? How effective was it?*

A strong conclusion will drive home the aim of the whole sermon and provide a strong motivation not only to receive and understand what the biblical text is saying but also to put its significance into practice in our lives.

Section 2: Interpretation

1. *Was the text properly understood and expounded? Did the main points of the text come across clearly?*

Was the meaning of the text explained adequately, especially the more difficult parts? As it was expounded, did the hearers have a sense of how it fit together—its integrity and purpose?

2. *Was the text set in its immediate, book, and whole Bible contexts? How did that help to clarify the contents?*

Have the listeners been helped to understand the significance of the passage and why it is an important word from God to our minds and hearts so many centuries later?

3. *Did the application arise from the text and reflect its main points?*

We want to ensure that the application has not been imposed on the text—brought in from the outside. Was there a smooth transition from the original hearers then to us now?

Section 3: Presentation

1. Was the sermon clear and easy to follow?

Good preaching is intellectually stimulating, but it is not complex or abstract. Were the main points stated clearly, explained lucidly, and applied cogently? Were the connections between the sections of the sermon explained well so that there was no loss of purpose or direction as the sermon unfolded?

2. Were illustrations used effectively to deepen understanding or focus application, or did they distract?

Did the illustrations achieve their purpose in supporting the sermon's teaching? Consider examples where the illustrations were effective or ineffective and try to work out why.

3. Was the sermon compelling? What response was asked for?

This is less about content and more about the preacher's style. The preacher will be in the foreground and our attitude toward him will determine our attitude toward the whole sermon.

4. How appropriate were the preacher's manner, verbal style, use of language, pitch and pace, and body language?

Each of these aspects should be considered, since any can heighten or diminish a sermon's usefulness.

Section 4: General

1. What was the strongest positive quality of the sermon?

Preachers need encouragement. They need to take away something from the critique that can act as a stimulus to work at developing strengths as well as resolving weaknesses.

2. What immediate steps could be taken to improve?

"Immediate steps" stresses the need to start somewhere in developing what is a lifelong improvement program. But the journey is long—and if the criticisms are too many or too negative it can be confusing and discouraging. Identify one or two clear changes or developments that the preacher can be encouraged to work on immediately. Try to end the session on a positive, hopeful, and prayerful note to increase the preacher's desire to be faithful and dependent on God who makes us grow.

General Index

Abraham, 24, 25, 77, 137, 179, 197–98, 211
Adam and Eve, 23, 208–9
Apollos, 18, 19
apostasy, 130, 146
apostolic authority, 67, 82
application. *See under* sermon
assurance (of salvation), 70, 115–16, 126, 130, 228
atonement, 116, 131–32
Augustine, 78

baptism
of believers, 210
of Jesus, 28–29, 116–17
Bible. *See also* Scripture(s)
biblical tones, 182–89
commentaries, 51, 52, 105, 136, 146, 171
dictionary, 52
expository preaching driven by the, 12–14
as God's self-revelation, 200
biblical sexual ethics, 55
"bolt-on" applications, 157–58
Brooks, Phillips, 15, 181
Brooks, Thomas, 135
bridge building (between the testaments), 200–202
Bunyan, John, 90

Calvin, John, 17–18
celebrity models of ministry, 44–45

church(es)
on facing the challenges in, 37–39
the responsibility of every, 34
commentaries, 51, 52, 105, 136, 146, 171
context
book, 122, 127–30
historical context, 53–54
immediate, 122, 125–27
whole Bible, 122, 130–33
contextualization, 55, 79, 173–74
continuity and discontinuity between the testaments, 200–202
creeds and Reformation confessions, 42
cultural differences (between biblical and modern times), 55–56
culture, 35–37, 46–47

David, 30, 77, 107, 148, 187–88, 214–15
Demas, 67
devil, 84, 85, 105, 109, 117, 153, 220
Diotrephes, 67
divine revelation, 2, 3, 26, 122, 131, 138, 200

educational methods, 1, 36
Elijah, 215–16
Epistles, 81
exegesis (as a stage in sermon preparation), 50–53
exposition
essential convictions for, 106–8
as a stage in sermon preparation, 53–58
expository preaching, 11–21, 57–58

Scripture Index